BEST EVER
FAT FREE
COOKBOOK

BEST EVER
FAT FREE
COOKBOOK

DELICIOUS FOOD FOR
HEALTHY EATING

Anne Sheasby

Sebastian Kelly

First published in 1998 by Sebastian Kelly
2 Rectory Road, Oxford OX4 1BW

© Anness Publishing Limited 1998

Produced by Anness Publishing Limited
Hermes House, 88–89 Blackfriars Road, London SE1 8HA

This edition published in 1998 for Lifetime Distributors, Building G, 2 Hudson Avenue, Castle Hill NSW 2154
Ph: (02) 9634 1333   Fax: (02) 9634 5955

ISBN 1-84081-010-6

A CIP catalogue record for this book is available from the British Library

Publisher: Joanna Lorenz
Senior Editor: Linda Fraser
Designers: Sara Kidd, Siân Keogh

Front Cover: Lisa Tai, Designer; Thomas Odulate, Photographer; Helen Trent, Stylist;
Marie-Ange Lapierre, Home Economist

Photographers: Karl Adamson, Edward Allwright, Steve Baxter, James Duncan, Amanda Heywood, Don Last,
Patrick McLeavey, Michael Michaels, Thomas Odulate, Peter Reilly
Recipes: Catherine Atkinson, Carla Capalbo, Kit Chan, Roz Denny, Christine France, Linda Fraser, Shirley Gill,
Christine Ingram, Sue Maggs, Annie Nichols, Maggie Pannell, Laura Washburn, Stephen Wheeler
Home Economists: Kit Chan assisted by Lucy McKelvie, Kathryn Hawkins, Wendy Lee, Jane Stevenson, Elizabeth Wolf-Cohen
Stylists: Madeleine Brehaut, Hilary Guy, Jo Harris, Blake Minton, Thomas Odulate, Kirsty Rawlings, Fiona Tillett

Previously published as part of a larger compendium: *The Ultimate Fat-Free Cookbook*

Printed in Hong Kong/China

1 3 5 7 9 10 8 6 4 2

NOTES
For all recipes, quantities are given in both metric and imperial measures and, where appropriate, measures are
given in standard cups and spoons. Follow one set, but not a mixture, because they are not interchangeable.

Standard spoon and cup measurements are level.
1 tsp = 5ml, 1 tbsp = 15ml; 1 cup = 250ml/8fl oz

Australian standard tablespoons are 20ml. Australian readers should use 3 tsp in place of 1 tbsp
for measuring small quantities of gelatine, cornflour, salt etc.

CONTENTS

~

INTRODUCTION

Government warnings, magazines and television constantly bombard us with the message that most of us eat too much fat and that this can be very damaging to our health, leading at best to overweight and at worst to fatal diseases. Yet cutting down on fat is not always easy and you can often end up with bland, unexciting and, frankly, disappointing meals. This book changes all that. It is packed with irresistible recipes from soups to pancakes and from barbecues to cakes – all low in fat.

Of course, some fat is essential in our diets to ensure that our bodies function properly. However, a regime rich in cream, cheese, butter and fatty meats is not healthy. Changing our approach to what we eat and how we cook it can, literally, be vital. The right sorts of fat in the right sorts of quantities will soon pay dividends in how you feel and how you look.

The easy-to-follow recipes in this book have been specially developed to fit into modern nutritional guidelines – and to be enjoyable. Each one has at-a-glance nutritional information, so you can instantly check the calories, fat and saturated fat content. The recipes are very low in fat – all contain less than 5 grams of fat per serving and many have even fewer.

Six chapters offer an extensive collection of recipes to suit all occasions: Soups, Starters & Snacks; Midweek Meals; Special Occasions; Vegetables & Salads; Desserts; and Cakes, Bakes & Cookies. In addition, the book starts with useful hints and tips on cooking with fat free and low fat ingredients and techniques. Fat free cooking has never been so painless.

FAT FREE GUIDELINES

The fats in food are made up of blocks of fatty acids and glycerol. Fatty acids are made up of chains of carbon atoms. How these chains are linked defines the type of fat: saturated, polyunsaturated or monounsaturated. All three types are present, in different proportions, in all the food we eat.

TYPES OF FAT

When carbon atoms in the fatty acids have no free bonds to link with other atoms, the fat is saturated. The body finds it hard to process and stores it as fat. Saturated fats raise cholesterol levels in the bloodstream and this may increase the risk of heart disease. Reducing our intake of saturated fats is the first step towards a healthier diet.

Saturated fats are usually solid at room temperature. Their main sources are animal products, such as meat and butter, but some are found in vegetable products, notably palm and coconut oil. Also, vegetable products that are labelled "hydrogenated vegetable oil" have been processed so that some of the unsaturated fatty acids have been converted to saturated.

Polyunsaturated fats are usually liquid at room temperature. There are two types: omega 6 from vegetable sources, such as sunflower oil and soft margarine, and omega 3 from oily fish, such as mackerel. A small intake of these is essential for health and they are thought to help reduce cholesterol levels.

Monounsaturated fats, too, are usually liquid at room temperature and are mainly of vegetable origin. They are found in foods such as olive oil and almonds and also oily fish. They are thought to help reduce cholesterol levels.

CUTTING DOWN ON FATS

Fats are a concentrated source of energy, but for a healthy diet, the daily intake should not exceed 30 per cent of total calories. Of an average total daily intake of 2, 000 calories, only 600 should be supplied by fats. One gram of fat supplies 9 calories, so the maximum daily intake should be no more than 66.6 grams. Saturated fats should form no more than 10 per cent of the total calories.

It is fairly easy to cut down on the most obvious sources of fats, such as butter, cream, full-fat milk and cheese, fatty meat and meat products, pastries and rich cakes. However, you should watch out for "hidden" fats in such products as biscuits and nuts, as well as in many canned processed foods. Even lean meats with the fat trimmed may contain as much as 10 per cent fat.

REDUCED FAT ALTERNATIVES

• Try replacing butter, margarine and hard fats with low fat spreads or polyunsaturated margarine. Even better for sandwiches and toast, replace them with fat free spreads, such as reduced sugar jams and marmalades, yeast extract, low fat soft cheese or fat free mayonnaise. Use polyunsaturated or monounsaturated vegetable oils for cooking. Spray oil helps control how much fat you are using for frying.
• Cut down your intake of high fat meat products, such as sausages, pies and pâtés. Replace with reduced fat products, lean meat and fish.
• Consider making your own salad dressings with low fat yogurt or fromage frais, instead of using full fat mayonnaise or salad cream.
• Replace snacks, such as crisps and biscuits, with fresh or dried fruits, vegetable sticks or low fat breadsticks.
• Rather than making gravies with meat cooking juices, use vegetable water or fat free stock.
• From time to time, substitute Quorn or tofu for meat in curries and other strong-flavoured recipes.
• When serving vegetables, sprinkle them with chopped fresh herbs or ground spices rather than adding a knob of butter.
• Substitute semi-skimmed or skimmed milk and milk products for full fat dairy products and use low fat yogurt or crème fraîche instead of cream.
• When buying canned fish such as tuna, choose it canned in brine rather than in oil.
• Substitute fruit juice, wine, beer or fat free stock for fats when cooking.
• To avoid low fat cooking becoming bland, be imaginative with flavourings, such as herbs, spices, soy sauce and wine.

Left: Many varieties of fish and seafood contain less than 1 gram of fat per 100 g/4 oz and they are perfect for fat free cooking methods.

It is worth investing in heavy-based or good quality non-stick pans, as you will find that you require far less fat when cooking.

• Always trim any visible fat and skin from all cuts of meat before cooking.
• When roasting or grilling meat, place it on a rack so that the fat drains off.
• Use heavy-based or non-stick cookware for frying so that you can use the minimum amount of fat. Dry fry meat to brown it when making casseroles and meat sauces.
• Poaching is an easy, delicious and fat free method of cooking chicken and fish.
• Steaming is one of the healthiest ways of cooking vegetables, chicken and fish, with the added bonus of preserving their colour and texture.

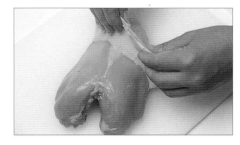

Above: Pulling off chicken and turkey skin and any loose fat directly underneath it before cooking dramatically reduces its fat content.

LOW-FAT FOODS

The following common foods have less than 1 gram of fat per 115 g/ 4 oz of food:

apples	lemon sole, raw
bananas	mushrooms
broccoli	onions
butter beans,	oranges
canned	peaches
cabbage	pears
carrots	peas
cauliflower	potatoes
cod fillets, raw	prawns
cornflakes	red kidney
courgettes	beans, canned
crab, canned	red lentils,
cucumber	cooked
dried mixed	skimmed milk
fruit	skimmed milk
egg white	soft cheese
fromage frais,	sugar, white
very low fat	tomatoes
grapefruit	tuna canned in
haddock, raw	brine
honey	yogurt, plain,
jam	low fat

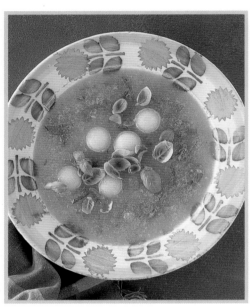

SOUPS,
STARTERS &
SNACKS

CHICKEN AND PASTA SOUP

INGREDIENTS

Serves 4–6

900ml/1½ pints/3¾ cups chicken stock
1 bay leaf
4 spring onions, sliced
225g/8oz button mushrooms, sliced
115g/4oz cooked chicken breast
50g/2oz soup pasta
150ml/¼ pint/⅔ cup dry white wine
15ml/1 tbsp chopped fresh parsley
salt and black pepper

NUTRITION NOTES

Per portion:

Energy	126Kcals/529kJ
Fat	2.2g
Saturated Fat	0.6g
Cholesterol	19mg
Fibre	1.3g

1 Put the stock and bay leaf into a pan and bring to the boil.

2 Add the spring onions and mushrooms to the stock.

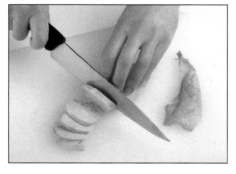

3 Remove the skin from the chicken and slice the meat thinly using a sharp knife. Add to the soup and season to taste. Heat through for about 2–3 minutes.

4 Add the pasta, cover and simmer for 7–8 minutes. Just before serving, add the wine and chopped parsley, heat through for 2–3 minutes, then season to taste.

CHICKEN AND COCONUT SOUP

This aromatic soup is rich with coconut milk and intensely flavoured with galangal, lemon grass and kaffir lime leaves.

— INGREDIENTS —

Serves 4–6
750ml/1¼ pints/3 cups coconut milk
475ml/16fl oz/2 cups chicken stock
4 lemon grass stalks, bruised and
   chopped
2.5cm/1in section galangal, thinly sliced
10 black peppercorns, crushed
10 kaffir lime leaves, torn
300g/11oz boneless chicken, cut into
   thin strips
115g/4oz button mushrooms
50g/2oz baby sweetcorn
60ml/4 tbsp lime juice
about 45ml/3 tbsp fish sauce
2 fresh chillies, seeded and chopped,
   chopped spring onions, and coriander
   leaves, to garnish

1 Bring the coconut milk and chicken stock to the boil. Add the lemon grass, galangal, peppercorns and half the kaffir lime leaves. Reduce the heat and simmer gently for 10 minutes.

2 Strain the stock into a clean pan. Return to the heat, then add the chicken, button mushrooms and baby sweetcorn. Simmer for 5–7 minutes or until the chicken is cooked.

3 Stir in the lime juice, fish sauce to taste and the rest of the lime leaves. Serve hot, garnished with chillies, spring onions and coriander.

NUTRITION NOTES	
Per portion:	
Energy	125Kcals/528kJ
Fat	3.03g
Saturated Fat	1.06g
Cholesterol	32.5mg
Fibre	0.4g

HOT AND SOUR PRAWN SOUP

This is a classic Thai seafood soup and is probably the most popular and well known soup from Thailand.

— INGREDIENTS —

Serves 4–6
450g/1lb king prawns
1 litre/1¾ pints/4 cups chicken stock
3 lemon grass stalks
10 kaffir lime leaves, torn in half
225g/8oz can straw mushrooms,
   drained
45ml/3 tbsp fish sauce
50ml/2fl oz/¼ cup lime juice
30ml/2 tbsp chopped spring onions
15ml/1 tbsp coriander leaves
4 fresh chillies, seeded and chopped
salt and black pepper

1 Shell and devein the prawns and set aside. Rinse the prawn shells, place them in a large saucepan with the stock and bring to the boil.

2 Bruise the lemon grass stalks with the blunt edge of a chopping knife and add them to the stock together with half the lime leaves. Simmer gently for 5–6 minutes, until the stalks change colour and the stock is fragrant.

NUTRITION NOTES	
Per portion:	
Energy	49Kcals/209kJ
Fat	0.45g
Saturated Fat	0.07g
Cholesterol	78.8mg
Fibre	0.09g

3 Strain the stock, return to the saucepan and reheat. Add the mushrooms and prawns, then cook until the prawns turn pink. Stir in the fish sauce, lime juice, spring onions, coriander, chillies and the rest of the lime leaves. Taste the soup and adjust the seasoning – it should be sour, salty, spicy and hot.

CREAMY COD CHOWDER

A delicious light version of a classic, this chowder is a tasty combination of smoked fish, vegetables, fresh herbs and milk. To cut the calories and stock even more, use vegetable or fish stock in place of the milk. Serve as a substantial starter or snack, or as a light main meal accompanied by warm crusty wholemeal bread.

INGREDIENTS

Serves 4–6
350g/12oz smoked cod fillet
1 small onion, finely chopped
1 bay leaf
4 black peppercorns
900ml/1½ pints/3¾ cups skimmed milk
10ml/2 tsp cornflour
200g/7oz canned sweetcorn kernels
15ml/1 tbsp chopped fresh parsley

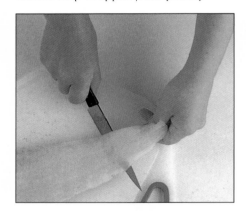

1 Skin the fish and put it into a large saucepan with the onion, bay leaf and peppercorns. Pour over the milk.

2 Bring to the boil, then reduce the heat and simmer very gently for 12–15 minutes, or until the fish is just cooked. Do not overcook.

3 Using a slotted spoon, lift out the fish and flake into large chunks. Remove the bay leaf and peppercorns and discard.

4 Blend the cornflour with 10ml/2 tsp cold water and add to the saucepan. Bring to the boil and simmer for about 1 minute or until slightly thickened.

5 Drain the sweetcorn kernels and add to the saucepan together with the flaked fish and parsley. Reheat gently and serve.

COOK'S TIP
The flavour of the chowder improves if it is made a day in advance. Leave to cool, then chill in the fridge until required. Reheat gently. Do not allow the soup to boil, or the fish will disintegrate.

NUTRITION NOTES

Per portion:
Energy	200Kcals/840kJ
Protein	24.71g
Fat	1.23g
Saturated Fat	0.32g

Italian Vegetable Soup

The success of this clear soup depends on the quality of the stock, so for the best results, be sure you use home-made vegetable stock rather than stock cubes.

INGREDIENTS

Serves 4
1 small carrot
1 baby leek
1 celery stick
50g/2oz green cabbage
900ml/1½ pints/3¾ cups vegetable stock
1 bay leaf
115g/4oz/1 cup cooked cannellini or
   haricot beans
25g/1oz/⅕ cup soup pasta, such as tiny
   shells, bows, stars or elbows
salt and black pepper
snipped fresh chives, to garnish

1 Cut the carrot, leek and celery into 5cm/2in long julienne strips. Slice the cabbage very finely.

NUTRITION NOTES

Per portion:	
Energy	69Kcals/288kJ
Protein	3.67g
Fat	0.71g
Saturated Fat	0.05g
Fibre	2.82g

2 Put the stock and bay leaf into a large saucepan and bring to the boil. Add the carrot, leek and celery, cover and simmer for 6 minutes.

3 Add the cabbage, beans and pasta shapes. Stir, then simmer uncovered for a further 4–5 minutes, or until the vegetables and pasta are tender.

4 Remove the bay leaf and season with salt and pepper to taste. Ladle into four soup bowls and garnish with snipped chives. Serve immediately.

CARROT AND CORIANDER SOUP

Nearly all root vegetables make excellent soups as they purée well and have an earthy flavour which complements the sharper flavours of herbs and spices. Carrots are particularly versatile, and this simple soup is elegant in both flavour and appearance.

INGREDIENTS

Serves 6
10ml/2 tsp sunflower oil
1 onion, chopped
1 celery stick, sliced, plus 2–3 leafy
  celery tops
2 small potatoes, chopped
450g/1lb carrots, preferably young and
  tender, chopped
1 litre/1¾ pints/4 cups chicken stock
10–15ml/2–3 tsp ground coriander
15ml/1 tbsp chopped fresh coriander
200ml/7fl oz/1 cup semi-skimmed milk
salt and black pepper

1 Heat the oil in a large flameproof casserole or heavy-based saucepan and fry the onion over a gentle heat for 3–4 minutes until slightly softened but not browned. Add the celery and potato, cook for a few minutes, then add the carrot. Fry over a gentle heat for 3–4 minutes, stirring frequently, and then cover. Reduce the heat even further and cook for about 10 minutes. Shake the pan or stir occasionally so the vegetables do not stick to the base.

2 Add the stock, bring to the boil and then partially cover and simmer for a further 8–10 minutes until the carrot and potato are tender.

3 Remove 6–8 tiny celery leaves for a garnish and finely chop about 15ml/1 tbsp of the remaining celery tops. In a small saucepan, dry fry the ground coriander for about 1 minute, stirring constantly. Reduce the heat, add the chopped celery and fresh coriander and fry for about 1 minute. Set aside.

4 Process the soup in a food processor or blender and pour into a clean saucepan. Stir in the milk, coriander mixture and seasoning. Heat gently, taste and adjust the seasoning. Serve garnished with the reserved celery.

NUTRITION NOTES

Per portion:
Energy	76.5Kcals/320kJ
Fat	3.2g
Saturated fat	0.65g
Cholesterol	2.3mg
Fibre	2.2g

COOK'S TIP
For a more piquant flavour, add a little freshly squeezed lemon juice just before serving. The contrast between the orange-coloured soup and the green garnish is a feast for the eye as well as the tastebuds.

MELON AND BASIL SOUP

A deliciously refreshing, chilled fruit soup, just right for a hot summer's day. It takes next to no time to prepare, leaving you free to enjoy the sunshine and, even better, it is almost totally fat-free.

INGREDIENTS

Serves 4–6
2 Charentais or rock melons
75g/3oz/6 tbsp caster sugar
175ml/6fl oz/³⁄₄ cup water
finely grated rind and juice of 1 lime
45ml/3 tbsp shredded fresh basil
fresh basil leaves, to garnish

1 Cut the melons in half across the middle. Scrape out the seeds and discard. Using a melon baller, scoop out 20–24 balls and set aside for the garnish. Scoop out the remaining flesh and place in a blender or food processor. Set aside.

2 Place the sugar, water and lime zest in a small pan over a low heat. Stir until dissolved, bring to the boil and simmer for 2–3 minutes. Remove from the heat and leave to cool slightly. Pour half the mixture into the blender or food processor with the melon flesh. Blend until smooth, adding the remaining syrup and lime juice to taste.

3 Pour the mixture into a bowl, stir in the basil and chill. Serve garnished with basil leaves and melon balls.

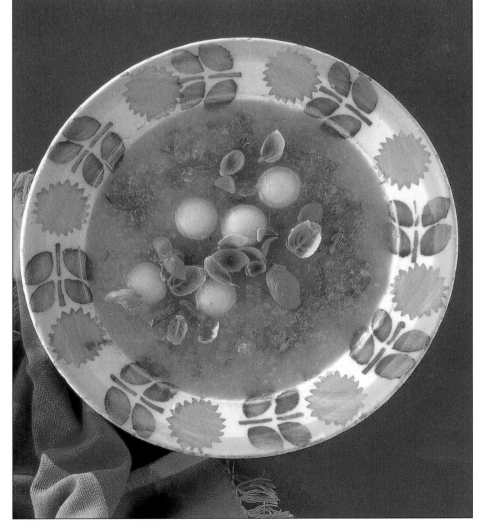

NUTRITION NOTES

Per portion:

Energy	69Kcals/293.8kJ
Fat	0.14g
Saturated Fat	0
Cholesterol	0
Fibre	0.47g

COOK'S TIP
Add the syrup in two stages, as the amount of sugar needed will depend on the sweetness of the melon.

PARMA HAM AND PEPPER PIZZAS

The delicious flavours of these
easy pizzas are hard to beat.

— INGREDIENTS —

Makes 4
½ loaf ciabatta bread
1 red pepper, roasted and peeled
1 yellow pepper, roasted and peeled
4 slices Parma ham, cut into
  thick strips
50g/2oz reduced fat mozzarella cheese
black pepper
tiny basil leaves, to garnish

— NUTRITION NOTES —

Per portion:	
Energy	93Kcals/395kJ
Fat	3.25g
Saturated Fat	1.49g
Cholesterol	14mg
Fibre	1g

1 Cut the bread into four thick slices
and toast until golden.

2 Cut the roasted peppers into thick
strips and arrange on the toasted
bread with the strips of Parma ham.
Preheat the grill.

3 Thinly slice the mozzarella and
arrange on top, then grind over
plenty of black pepper. Grill for 2–3
minutes until the cheese is bubbling.

4 Scatter the basil leaves on top and
serve immediately.

MELON WITH WILD STRAWBERRIES

This fragrant, colourful starter is the perfect way to begin a rich meal as both melons and strawberries are virtually fat-free. Here several varieties are combined with strongly flavoured wild or woodland strawberries. If wild strawberries are not available, use ordinary strawberries or raspberries instead.

INGREDIENTS

Serves 4
1 cantaloupe or Charentais melon
1 Galia melon
900g/2lb watermelon
175g/6oz wild strawberries
4 sprigs fresh mint, to garnish

NUTRITION NOTES

Per portion:
Energy	42.5Kcals/178.6kJ
Fat	0.32g
Saturated Fat	0
Cholesterol	0
Fibre	1.09g

1 Using a large sharp knife, cut all three melons in half.

2 Scoop out the seeds from both the cantaloupe or Charentais and Galia melons with a spoon.

3 With a melon scoop, take out as many balls as you can from all three melons. Combine in a large bowl and chill for at least 1 hour.

4 Add the wild strawberries and mix together gently. Spoon out into four stemmed glass dishes.

5 Garnish each of the melon salads with a small sprig of mint and serve at once.

COOK'S TIP
Ripe melons should give slightly when pressed at the base, and should give off a sweet scent. Buy carefully if you plan to use the fruit on the day. If one or more varieties of melon aren't available, then substitute another, or buy two or three of the same variety – the salad might not be quite so colourful, but it will taste equally refreshing.

MIDWEEK
MEALS

PASTA WITH CHICK-PEA SAUCE

This is a delicious, and very speedy, low fat dish. The quality of canned pulses and tomatoes is so good that it is possible to transform them into a very fresh tasting pasta sauce in minutes. Choose whatever pasta shapes you like, although hollow shapes, such as penne (quills) or shells are particularly good with this sauce.

INGREDIENTS

Serves 6

450g/1lb penne or other pasta shapes
30ml/2 tsp olive oil
1 onion, thinly sliced
1 red pepper, seeded and sliced
400g/14oz can chopped tomatoes
425g/15oz can chick-peas
30ml/2 tbsp dry vermouth (optional)
5ml/1 tsp dried oregano
1 large bay leaf
30ml/2 tbsp capers
salt and black pepper
fresh oregano, to garnish

COOK'S TIP
Choose fresh or dried unfilled pasta for this dish. Whichever you choose, cook it in a large saucepan of water, so that the pasta keeps separate and doesn't stick together. Fresh pasta takes about 2–4 minutes to cook and dried pasta about 8–10 minutes. Cook pasta until it is *al dente* – firm and neither too hard nor too soft.

NUTRITION NOTES

Per portion:
Energy	268Kcals/1125kJ
Fat	2.0g
Saturated Fat	0.5g
Cholesterol	1.3mg
Fibre	4.3g

1 Boil the pasta as instructed on the packet, then drain. Meanwhile, heat the oil in a large saucepan and gently fry the onion and pepper for about 5 minutes, stirring occasionally, until softened.

2 Add the tomatoes, chick-peas with their liquid, vermouth (if liked), herbs and capers and stir well.

3 Season to taste and bring to the boil, then simmer for about 10 minutes. Remove the bay leaf and mix in the pasta. Reheat and serve hot, garnished with sprigs of oregano.

TAGLIATELLE WITH MILANESE SAUCE

INGREDIENTS

Serves 4

1 onion, finely chopped
1 celery stick, finely chopped
1 red pepper, seeded and diced
1–2 garlic cloves, crushed
150ml/¼ pint/⅔ cup vegetable or
   chicken stock
400g/14oz can tomatoes
15ml/1 tbsp tomato purée
10ml/2 tsp caster sugar
5ml/1 tsp mixed dried herbs
350g/12oz tagliatelle
115g/4oz button mushrooms, sliced
60ml/4 tbsp dry white wine
115g/4oz lean cooked ham, diced
salt and black pepper
15ml/1 tbsp chopped fresh parsley,
   to garnish

1 Put the chopped onion, celery, pepper and garlic into a saucepan. Add the stock, bring to the boil and cook for 5 minutes or until tender.

COOK'S TIP

To reduce the calorie and fat content even more, omit the ham and use sweetcorn kernels or cooked broccoli florets instead.

2 Add the tomatoes, tomato purée, sugar and herbs. Season with salt and pepper. Bring to the boil and simmer for 30 minutes stirring occasionally, until the sauce is thick.

3 Cook the pasta in a large pan of boiling, salted water according to the packet instructions, until al dente. Drain thoroughly.

4 Put the mushrooms into a pan with the white wine, cover and cook for 3–4 minutes until the mushrooms are tender and all the wine has been absorbed.

5 Stir the mushrooms and ham into the tomato sauce and reheat gently over a low heat.

6 Transfer the pasta to a warmed serving dish and spoon on the sauce. Garnish with parsley.

NUTRITION NOTES

Per portion:

Energy	405Kcals/1700kJ
Fat	3.5g
Saturated Fat	0.8g
Cholesterol	17mg
Fibre	4.5g

MUSHROOM AND OKRA CURRY

This simple but delicious curry with its fresh gingery mango relish is best served with plain basmati rice.

INGREDIENTS

Serves 4

4 garlic cloves, roughly chopped
2.5cm/1in piece fresh root ginger, peeled and roughly chopped
1–2 red chillies, seeded and chopped
175ml/6fl oz/³⁄4 cup water
15ml/1 tbsp sunflower oil
5ml/1 tsp coriander seeds
5ml/1 tsp cumin seeds
5ml/1 tsp ground cumin
2 cardamom pods, seeds removed and crushed
pinch of ground turmeric
400g/14oz can chopped tomatoes
450g/1lb mushrooms, quartered if large
225g/8oz okra, trimmed and cut into 1cm/¹⁄2in slices
30ml/2 tbsp chopped fresh coriander
basmati rice, to serve

For the mango relish

1 large ripe mango, about 500g/1¹⁄4lb
1 small garlic clove, crushed
1 onion, finely chopped
10ml/2 tsp grated fresh root ginger
1 fresh red chilli, seeded and finely chopped
pinch of salt and sugar

1 For the mango relish, peel the mango and then cut off the fruit from the stone. Put the mango into a bowl and mash with a fork, or use a food processor.

2 Add the rest of the relish ingredients to the mango, mix well and set aside.

3 Place the garlic, ginger, chillies and 45ml/3 tbsp of the water into a blender and blend until smooth. Heat the oil in a large pan. Add the coriander and cumin seeds and allow them to sizzle for a few seconds, then add the ground cumin, cardamom seeds and turmeric and cook for 1 minute more.

4 Add the paste from the blender, the tomatoes, remaining water, mushrooms and okra. Stir and bring to the boil. Reduce the heat, cover and simmer for 5 minutes. Uncover, turn up the heat slightly and cook for another 5–10 minutes until the okra is tender. Stir in the fresh coriander and serve with rice and the mango relish.

NUTRITION NOTES	
Per portion:	
Energy	139Kcals/586kJ
Fat	4.6g
Saturated Fat	0.63g
Cholesterol	0
Fibre	6.96g

LENTIL BOLOGNESE

A really useful sauce to serve with pasta, as a pancake stuffing or even as a protein-packed sauce for vegetables.

INGREDIENTS

Serves 6
45ml/3 tbsp olive oil
1 onion, chopped
2 garlic cloves, crushed
2 carrots, coarsely grated
2 celery sticks, chopped
115g/4oz/²/₃ cup red lentils
400g/14oz can chopped tomatoes
30ml/2 tbsp tomato purée
450ml/³/₄ pint/2 cups stock
15ml/1 tbsp fresh marjoram, chopped, or 5ml/1 tsp dried marjoram
salt and black pepper

1 Heat the oil in a large saucepan and gently fry the onion, garlic, carrots and celery for about 5 minutes, until they are soft.

NUTRITION NOTES

Per portion:	
Energy	103Kcals/432kJ
Fat	2.19g
Saturated Fat	0.85g
Fibre	2.15g

2 Add the lentils, tomatoes, tomato purée, stock, marjoram and seasoning to the pan.

3 Bring the mixture to the boil, then partially cover with a lid and simmer for 20 minutes until thick and soft. Use the sauce as required.

COOK'S TIP
You can easily reduce the fat in this recipe by using less olive oil, or substituting a little of the stock and cooking the vegetables over a low heat in a non-stick frying pan until they are soft.

VEGETARIAN CASSOULET

Every town in south-west France has its own version of this popular classic. Warm French bread is all that you need to accompany this hearty low fat vegetable version.

INGREDIENTS

Serves 4–6
400g/14oz/2 cups dried haricot beans
1 bay leaf
2 onions
3 whole cloves
2 garlic cloves, crushed
5ml/1 tsp olive oil
2 leeks, thickly sliced
12 baby carrots
115g/4oz button mushrooms
400g/14oz can chopped tomatoes
15ml/1 tbsp tomato purée
5ml/1 tsp paprika
15ml/1 tbsp chopped fresh thyme
30ml/2 tbsp chopped fresh parsley
115g/4oz/2 cups fresh white
    breadcrumbs
salt and black pepper

NUTRITION NOTES

Per portion:
Energy	325Kcals/1378kJ
Fat	3.08g
Saturated Fat	0.46g
Cholesterol	0
Fibre	15.68g

COOK'S TIP
If you're short of time, use canned haricot beans – you'll need two 400g/14oz cans. Drain, reserving the bean juices and make up to 400ml/14fl oz/1²/₃ cups with vegetable stock.

1 Soak the beans overnight in plenty of cold water. Drain and rinse under cold running water. Put them in a saucepan with 1.75 litres/3 pints/ 7½ cups of cold water and the bay leaf. Bring to the boil and cook rapidly for 10 minutes.

2 Peel one of the onions and spike with the cloves. Add to the beans, then reduce the heat. Cover and simmer gently for 1 hour, until the beans are almost tender. Drain, reserving the stock but discarding the bay leaf and onion.

3 Chop the remaining onion and put it into a large flameproof casserole together with the crushed garlic and olive oil. Cook gently for 5 minutes, or until softened.

4 Preheat the oven to 160°C/325°F/ Gas 3. Add the leeks, carrots, mushrooms, chopped tomatoes, tomato purée, paprika and thyme to the casserole, then pour in about 400ml/14fl oz/1²/₃ cups of the reserved stock.

5 Bring to the boil, cover and simmer gently for 10 minutes. Stir in the cooked beans and parsley. Season to taste with salt and pepper.

6 Sprinkle the breadcrumbs over the top and bake uncovered for 35 minutes or until the topping is golden brown and crisp.

TURKEY AND TOMATO HOT POT

Here, turkey is turned into tasty meatballs in a rich tomato sauce.

INGREDIENTS

Serves 4

25g/1oz white bread, crusts removed
30ml/2 tbsp skimmed milk
1 garlic clove, crushed
2.5ml/¹/₂ tsp caraway seeds
225g/8oz minced turkey
1 egg white
350ml/12fl oz/1¹/₂ cups chicken stock
400g/14oz can tomatoes
15ml/1 tbsp tomato purée
90g/3¹/₂oz/¹/₂ cup easy-cook rice
salt and black pepper
fresh basil, to garnish
carrot and courgette ribbons, to serve

1 Cut the bread into small cubes and put into a mixing bowl. Sprinkle over the milk and leave to soak for 5 minutes.

2 Add the garlic clove, caraway seeds, turkey and seasoning to the bread. Mix together well.

3 Whisk the egg white until stiff, then fold, half at a time, into the turkey mixture. Chill for 10 minutes.

4 While the turkey mixture is chilling, put the stock, tomatoes and tomato purée into a large saucepan and bring to the boil.

5 Add the rice, stir and cook briskly for about 5 minutes. Turn the heat down to a gentle simmer.

6 Meanwhile, shape the turkey mixture into 16 small balls. Carefully drop them into the tomato stock and simmer for a further 8–10 minutes, or until both the turkey balls and rice are cooked. Garnish with basil, and serve with carrot and courgette ribbons.

COOK'S TIPS

To make carrot and courgette ribbons, cut the vegetables lengthways into thin strips using a vegetable peeler, and blanch or steam until lightly cooked.

Lean minced turkey is low in fat and is a good source of protein. It makes an ideal base for this tasty low fat supper dish. Use minced chicken in place of turkey for an appetizing alternative.

NUTRITION NOTES

Per portion:

Energy	190Kcals/798kJ
Protein	18.04g
Fat	1.88g
Saturated Fat	0.24g
Fibre	10.4g

Turkey and Macaroni Cheese

A tasty low fat alternative to macaroni cheese, the addition of turkey rashers ensures this dish is a family favourite. Serve with warm ciabatta bread and a mixed leaf salad.

Nutrition Notes

Per portion:
Energy	152Kcals/637kJ
Fat	2.8g
Saturated Fat	0.7g
Cholesterol	12mg
Fibre	1.1g

Ingredients

Serves 4

1 medium onion, chopped
150ml/¼ pint/⅔ cup vegetable or chicken stock
25g/1oz/2 tbsp low fat margarine
45ml/3 tbsp plain flour
300ml/½ pint/1¼ cup skimmed milk
50g/2oz reduced fat Cheddar cheese, grated
5ml/1 tsp dry mustard
225g/8oz quick-cook macaroni
4 smoked turkey rashers, cut in half
2–3 firm tomatoes, sliced
a few fresh basil leaves
15ml/1 tbsp grated Parmesan cheese
salt and black pepper

1 Put the chopped onion and stock into a non-stick frying pan. Bring to the boil, stirring occasionally and cook for 5–6 minutes or until the stock has reduced entirely and the onion is transparent.

2 Put the margarine, flour, milk and seasoning into a saucepan and whisk together over the heat until thickened and smooth. Draw aside and add the cheese, mustard and onion.

3 Cook the macaroni in a large pan of boiling, salted water according to the instructions on the packet. Preheat the grill. Drain thoroughly and stir into the sauce. Transfer to a shallow oven-proof dish.

4 Arrange the turkey rashers and tomatoes overlapping on top of the macaroni cheese. Tuck in the basil leaves, then sprinkle with Parmesan and grill to lightly brown the top.

THAI CHICKEN AND VEGETABLE STIR-FRY

Serves 4

1 piece lemon grass (or the rind of
  ½ lemon)
1cm/½in piece fresh root ginger
1 large garlic clove
30ml/2 tbsp sunflower oil
275g/10oz lean chicken,
  thinly sliced
½ red pepper, seeded and
  sliced
½ green pepper, seeded and sliced
4 spring onions, chopped
2 medium carrots, cut into matchsticks
115g/4oz fine green beans
25g/1oz peanuts, lightly crushed
30 ml/2 tbsp oyster sauce
pinch of sugar
salt and black pepper
coriander leaves, to garnish

—— NUTRITION NOTES ——

Per portion:
Energy	106Kcals/449kJ
Fat	2.05g
Saturated Fat	1.10g
Cholesterol	1.10mg
Fibre	109g

1 Thinly slice the lemon grass or lemon rind. Peel and chop the ginger and garlic. Heat the oil in a frying pan over a high heat. Add the lemon grass or lemon rind, ginger and garlic, and stir-fry for 30 seconds until brown.

2 Add the chicken and stir-fry for 2 minutes. Then add all the vegetables and stir-fry for 4–5 minutes, until the chicken is cooked and the vegetables are almost cooked.

3 Finally, stir in the peanuts, oyster sauce, sugar and seasoning to taste. Stir-fry for another minute to blend the flavours. Serve at once, sprinkled with the coriander leaves and accompanied by rice.

COOK'S TIP
Make this quick supper dish a little hotter by adding more fresh root ginger, if liked.

TUNA AND MIXED VEGETABLE PASTA

— INGREDIENTS —

Serves 4

10ml/2 tsp olive oil
115g/4oz/1½ cups button
* mushrooms, sliced*
1 garlic clove, crushed
½ red pepper, seeded and chopped
15ml/1 tbsp tomato paste
300ml/½ pint/1¼ cups tomato juice
115g/4oz/1 cup frozen peas
15–30ml/1–2 tbsp drained pickled
* green peppercorns, crushed*
350g/12oz whole wheat pasta shapes
200g/7oz can tuna chunks in water,
* drained*
6 spring onions, diagonally sliced

1 Heat the oil in a pan and gently sauté the mushrooms, garlic and pepper until softened. Stir in the tomato paste, then add the tomato juice, peas and some or all of the crushed peppercorns, depending on how spicy you like the sauce. Bring to the boil, lower the heat and simmer.

2 Bring a large saucepan of lightly salted water to the boil and cook the pasta for about 12 minutes (or according to the instructions on the package), until just tender. When the pasta is almost ready, add the tuna to the sauce and heat through gently. Stir in the spring onions. Drain the pasta, turn it into a heated bowl and pour over the sauce. Toss to mix. Serve at once.

NUTRITION NOTES	
Per portion:	
Energy	354Kcals/1514kJ
Fat	4.5g
Saturated Fat	0.67g
Cholesterol	22.95mg
Fibre	10.35g

SWEET AND SOUR FISH

White fish is high in protein, vitamins and minerals, but low in fat. Serve this tasty, nutritious dish with brown rice and stir-fried cabbage or spinach for a delicious lunch.

— INGREDIENTS —

Serves 4

60ml/4 tbsp cider vinegar
45ml/3 tbsp light soy sauce
50g/2oz/¼ cup granulated sugar
15ml/1 tbsp tomato purée
25ml/1½ tbsp cornflour
250ml/8fl oz/1 cup water
1 green pepper, seeded and sliced
225g/8oz can pineapple pieces in
* fruit juice*
225g/8oz tomatoes, peeled and
* chopped*
225g/8oz/2 cups button mushrooms,
* sliced*
675g/1½lb chunky haddock fillets,
* skinned*
salt and black pepper

1 Preheat the oven to 180°C/350°F/ Gas 4. Mix together the vinegar, soy sauce, sugar and tomato purée in a saucepan. Put the cornflour in a jug, stir in the water, then add the mixture to the saucepan, stirring well. Bring to the boil, stirring constantly until thickened. Lower the heat and simmer the sauce for 5 minutes.

2 Add the green pepper, canned pineapple pieces (with juice) and tomatoes to the pan and stir well. Mix in the mushrooms and heat through. Season to taste with salt and pepper.

3 Place the fish in a single layer in a shallow ovenproof dish, spoon over the sauce and cover with foil. Bake for 15–20 minutes until the fish is tender. Serve immediately.

NUTRITION NOTES	
Per portion:	
Energy	255Kcals/1070kJ
Fat	2g
Saturated Fat	0.5g
Cholesterol	61mg

HOT SPICY PRAWNS WITH CAMPANELLE

This low fat prawn sauce tossed with hot pasta is an ideal supper-time dish. Add less or more chilli depending on how hot you like your food.

INGREDIENTS

Serves 4–6

225g/8oz tiger prawns, cooked
  and peeled
1–2 garlic cloves, crushed
finely grated rind of 1 lemon
15ml/1 tbsp lemon juice
1.5ml/¼ tsp red chilli paste or 1 large
  pinch of chilli powder
15ml/1 tbsp light soy sauce
150g/5oz smoked turkey rashers
1 shallot or small onion, finely chopped
60ml/4 tbsp dry white wine
225g/8oz campanelle or other
  pasta shapes
60ml/4 tbsp fish stock
4 firm ripe tomatoes, peeled, seeded
  and chopped
30ml/2 tbsp chopped fresh parsley
salt and black pepper

NUTRITION NOTES

Per portion:	
Energy	331Kcals/1388kJ
Fat	2.9g
Saturated Fat	0.6g
Cholesterol	64mg
Fibre	3.2g

COOK'S TIP
To save time later, the prawns and marinade ingredients can be mixed together, covered and chilled in the fridge overnight, until ready to use.

1 In a glass bowl, mix the prawns with the garlic, lemon rind and juice, chilli paste or powder and soy sauce. Season with salt and pepper, cover and marinate for at least 1 hour.

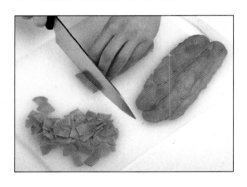

2 Grill the turkey rashers, then cut them into 5mm/¼in dice.

3 Put the shallot or onion and white wine into a pan, bring to the boil, cover and cook for 2–3 minutes or until they are tender and the wine has reduced by half.

4 Cook the pasta according to the packet instructions in a large pan of boiling, salted water until al dente. Drain thoroughly.

5 Just before serving, put the prawns with their marinade into a large frying pan, bring to the boil quickly and add the smoked turkey and fish stock. Heat through for 1 minute.

6 Add to the pasta with the chopped tomatoes and parsley, toss quickly and serve at once.

Herby Fishcakes with Lemon Sauce

The wonderful flavour of fresh herbs makes these fishcakes the catch of the day.

Ingredients

Serves 4

350g/12oz potatoes, roughly chopped
75ml/5 tbsp skimmed milk
350g/12oz haddock or hoki
    fillets, skinned
15ml/1 tbsp lemon juice
15ml/1 tbsp creamed horseradish sauce
30ml/2 tbsp chopped fresh parsley
flour, for dusting
115g/4oz/2 cups fresh wholemeal
    breadcrumbs
salt and black pepper
flat leaf parsley sprigs, to garnish
sugar snap peas or mange-tout and a
    sliced tomato and onion salad,
    to serve

For the lemon and chive sauce
thinly pared rind and juice of
    ½ small lemon
120ml/4fl oz/½ cup dry white wine
2 thin slices of fresh root ginger
10ml/2 tsp cornflour
30ml/2 tbsp snipped fresh chives

Nutrition Notes

Per portion:

Energy	232Kcals/975kJ
Protein	19.99g
Fat	1.99g
Saturated Fat	0.26g
Fibre	3.11g

Cook's Tip

Dry white wine is a tasty fat-free basis for this herby sauce. Try using cider as an alternative to wine, for a change.

1 Cook the potatoes in a large saucepan of boiling water for 15–20 minutes. Drain and mash with the milk and season to taste.

2 Purée the fish together with the lemon juice and horseradish sauce in a blender or food processor. Mix with the potatoes and parsley.

3 With floured hands, shape the mixture into eight fishcakes and coat with the breadcrumbs. Chill in the fridge for 30 minutes.

4 Preheat the grill to medium and cook the fishcakes for 5 minutes on each side, until browned.

5 To make the sauce, cut the lemon rind into juliénne strips and put into a large saucepan together with the lemon juice, wine and ginger. Season to taste with salt and pepper.

6 Simmer, uncovered, for about 6 minutes. Blend the cornflour with 15ml/1 tbsp of cold water, add to the pan and simmer until clear. Stir in the chives immediately before serving.

7 Serve the sauce hot with the fishcakes, garnished with parsley sprigs and accompanied with mange-tout and a tomato and onion salad.

MEDITERRANEAN FISH CUTLETS

These low fat fish cutlets are well complemented by boiled potatoes, broccoli and carrots.

INGREDIENTS

Serves 4

4 white fish cutlets, about 150g/5oz each

about 150ml/¼ pint/⅔ cup fish stock or dry white wine (or a mixture of the two), for poaching

1 bay leaf, a few black peppercorns and a strip of pared lemon rind, for flavouring

For the tomato sauce

400g/14oz can chopped tomatoes
1 garlic clove, crushed
15ml/1 tbsp pastis or other aniseed-flavoured liqueur
15ml/1 tbsp drained capers
12–16 stoned black olives
salt and black pepper

1 To make the sauce, place the chopped tomatoes, garlic, pastis or liqueur, capers and olives in a saucepan. Season to taste with salt and pepper and cook over a low heat for about 15 minutes, stirring occasionally.

2 Place the fish in a frying pan, pour over the stock and/or wine and add the bay leaf, peppercorns and lemon rind. Cover and simmer for 10 minutes or until it flakes easily.

3 Using a slotted spoon, transfer the fish into a heated dish. Strain the stock into the tomato sauce and boil to reduce slightly. Season the sauce, pour it over the fish and serve immediately, sprinkled with the chopped parsley.

COOK'S TIP
Remove skin from cutlets and reduce the quantity of olives to reduce calories and fat. Use 450g/1lb fresh tomatoes, skinned and chopped, in place of the canned tomatoes.

NUTRITION NOTES

Per portion:
Energy	165Kcals/685kJ
Fat	3.55g
Saturated Fat	0.5g
Cholesterol	69mg

PASTA PRIMAVERA

You can use any mixture of fresh, young spring vegetables to make this delicately flavoured pasta dish.

INGREDIENTS

Serves 4

225g/8oz thin asparagus spears, chopped in half
115g/4oz mange-tout, topped and tailed
115g/4oz baby sweetcorn
225g/8oz whole baby carrots, trimmed
1 small red pepper, seeded and chopped
8 spring onions, sliced
225g/8oz torchietti or other pasta shapes
150ml/¼ pint/⅔ cup low fat cottage cheese
150ml/¼ pint/⅔ cup low fat yogurt
15ml/1 tbsp lemon juice
15ml/1 tbsp chopped parsley
15ml/1 tbsp snipped chives
skimmed milk (optional)
salt and black pepper
sun-dried tomato bread, to serve

2 Cook the baby corn, carrots, red pepper and spring onions in the same way until tender. Drain and rinse.

4 Put the cottage cheese, yogurt, lemon juice, parsley, chives and seasoning into a food processor or blender and process until smooth. Thin the sauce with skimmed milk, if necessary. Put into a large pan with the pasta and vegetables, heat gently and toss carefully. Serve at once with sun-dried tomato bread.

1 Cook the asparagus spears in a pan of boiling, salted water for 3–4 minutes. Add the mange-tout halfway through the cooking time. Drain and rinse both under cold water to stop further cooking.

3 Cook the pasta in a large pan of boiling, salted water according to the packet instruction, until *al dente*. Drain thoroughly.

NUTRITION NOTES	
Per portion:	
Energy	320Kcals/1344kJ
Fat	3.1g
Saturated Fat	0.4g
Cholesterol	3mg
Fibre	6.2g

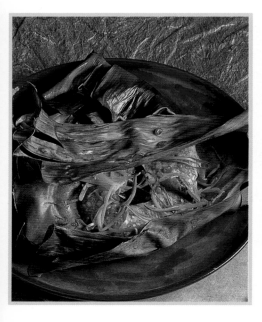

SPECIAL OCCASIONS

TOFU AND GREEN BEAN CURRY

This exotic curry is simple and quick to make. This recipe uses beans and mushrooms, but you can use almost any kind of vegetable such as aubergines, bamboo shoots or broccoli.

INGREDIENTS

Serves 4
350ml/12fl oz/1½ cups coconut milk
15ml/1 tbsp red curry paste
45ml/3 tbsp fish sauce
10ml/2 tsp sugar
225g/8oz button mushrooms
115g/4oz French beans, trimmed
175g/6oz bean curd, rinsed and cut into 2cm/¾in cubes
4 kaffir lime leaves, torn
2 red chillies, seeded and sliced
coriander leaves, to garnish

NUTRITION NOTES

Per portion:
Energy	100Kcals/420kJ
Fat	3.36g
Saturated Fat	0.48g
Cholesterol	0
Fibre	1.35g

1 Put about one third of the coconut milk in a wok or saucepan. Cook until it starts to separate and an oily sheen appears.

2 Add the red curry paste, fish sauce and sugar to the coconut milk. Mix together thoroughly.

3 Add the mushrooms. Stir and cook for 1 minute.

4 Stir in the rest of the coconut milk and bring back to the boil.

COOK'S TIP
Use 5–10ml/1–2 tsp hot chilli powder, if fresh red chillies aren't available. When preparing fresh chillies, wear rubber gloves and wash hands, work surfaces and utensils thoroughly afterwards. Chillies contain volatile oils which can irritate and burn sensitive areas, especially eyes.

5 Add the French beans and cubes of bean curd and simmer gently for another 4–5 minutes.

6 Stir in the kaffir lime leaves and chillies. Serve garnished with the coriander leaves.

RATATOUILLE PANCAKES

These pancakes are made slightly thicker than usual to hold the juicy vegetable filling. By using cooking spray, you can control the amount of fat you are using and keep it to a minimum.

INGREDIENTS

Serves 4
75g/3oz/⅔ cup plain flour
pinch of salt
25g/1oz/¼ cup medium oatmeal
1 egg
300ml/½ pint/1¼ cups skimmed milk
non-stick cooking spray
mixed salad, to serve

For the filling
1 large aubergine, cut into 2.5cm/
    1in cubes
1 garlic clove, crushed
2 medium courgettes, sliced
1 green pepper, seeded and sliced
1 red pepper, seeded and sliced
75ml/5 tbsp vegetable stock
200g/7oz can chopped tomatoes
5ml/1 tsp cornflour
salt and black pepper

NUTRITION NOTES

Per portion:
Energy	182Kcals/767kJ
Protein	9.36g
Fat	3.07g
Saturated Fat	0.62g
Fibre	4.73g

COOK'S TIP
Adding oatmeal to the batter mixture adds flavour, colour and texture to the cooked pancakes. If you like, wholemeal flour may be used in place of white flour to add extra fibre and flavour too.

1 Sift the flour and a pinch of salt into a bowl. Stir in the oatmeal. Make a well in the centre, add the egg and half the milk and mix to a smooth batter. Gradually beat in the remaining milk. Cover the bowl and leave to stand for 30 minutes.

2 Spray an 18cm/7in heavy-based frying pan with cooking spray. Heat the pan, then pour in just enough batter to cover the base of the pan thinly. Cook for 2–3 minutes, until the underside is golden brown. Flip over and cook for a further 1–2 minutes.

3 Slide the pancake out on to a plate lined with non-stick baking paper. Stack the other pancakes on top as they are made, interleaving each with non-stick baking paper. Keep warm.

4 For the filling, put the aubergine in a colander and sprinkle well with salt. Leave to stand on a plate for 30 minutes. Rinse thoroughly and drain well.

5 Put the garlic clove, courgettes, peppers, stock and tomatoes into a large saucepan. Simmer uncovered, stirring occasionally, for 10 minutes. Add the aubergine and cook for a further 15 minutes. Blend the cornflour with 10ml/2 tsp water and stir into the saucepan. Simmer for 2 minutes. Season to taste.

6 Spoon some of the ratatouille mixture into the middle of each pancake. Fold each one in half, then in half again to make a cone shape. Serve hot with a mixed salad.

AUTUMN GLORY

Glorious pumpkin shells summon up the delights of autumn and look too good to throw away, so use one as a serving pot. Pumpkin and pasta make marvellous partners, especially as a main course served from the baked shell.

INGREDIENTS

Serves 4–6
1 pumpkin, about 2kg/4–4¹⁄₂lb
1 onion, sliced
2.5cm/1in fresh root ginger
15ml/1 tbsp extra virgin olive oil
1 courgette, sliced
115g/4oz sliced mushrooms
400g/14oz can chopped tomatoes
75g/3oz/1 cup pasta shells
450ml/³⁄₄ pint/2 cups stock
60ml/4 tbsp fromage frais
30ml/2 tbsp chopped fresh basil
salt and black pepper

NUTRITION NOTES

Per portion (6 servings):
Energy	140Kcals/588kJ
Fat	4.29g
Saturated Fat	1.17g
Cholesterol	2.5mg
Fibre	4.45g

COOK'S TIP
Use reduced fat or very low fat fromage frais to cut the calories and fat. Cook the onion, ginger and pumpkin flesh in 30–45ml/ 2–3 tbsp vegetable stock in place of the oil, to cut the calories and fat more.

1 Preheat the oven to 180°C/350°F/ Gas 4. Cut the top off the pumpkin with a large sharp knife, then scoop out and discard the seeds.

2 Using a small sharp knife and a sturdy tablespoon, extract as much of the pumpkin flesh as possible, then chop it into chunks.

3 Bake the pumpkin shell with its lid on for 45 minutes to 1 hour until the inside begins to soften.

4 Meanwhile make the filling. Gently fry the onion, ginger and pumpkin chunks in the olive oil for about 10 minutes, stirring occasionally.

5 Add the courgette and mushrooms and cook for a further 3 minutes, then stir in the tomatoes, pasta shells and stock. Season well, bring to the boil, then cover and simmer gently for another 10 minutes.

6 Stir the fromage frais and basil into the pasta and spoon the mixture into the pumpkin. (It may not be possible to fit all the filling into the pumpkin shell; serve the rest separately if this is the case.)

PASTA WITH HERBY SCALLOPS

Low fat fromage frais, flavoured with mustard, garlic and herbs, makes a deceptively creamy sauce for pasta.

INGREDIENTS

Serves 4
120ml/4fl oz/½ cup low fat
  fromage frais
10ml/2 tsp wholegrain mustard
2 garlic cloves, crushed
30–45ml/2–3 tbsp fresh lime juice
60ml/4 tbsp chopped fresh parsley
30ml/2 tbsp snipped chives
350g/12oz black tagliatelle
12 large scallops
60ml/4 tbsp white wine
150ml/¼ pint/⅔ cup fish stock
salt and black pepper
lime wedges and parsley sprigs,
  to garnish

1 To make the sauce, mix the fromage frais, mustard, garlic, lime juice, parsley, chives and seasoning together in a mixing bowl.

2 Cook the pasta in a large pan of boiling salted water until *al dente*. Drain thoroughly.

3 Slice the scallops in half, horizontally. Keep any coral whole. Put the wine and fish stock into a saucepan and heat to simmering point. Add the scallops and cook very gently for 3–4 minutes. (Don't cook for any longer, or they will toughen.)

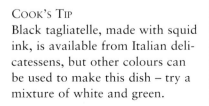

COOK'S TIP
Black tagliatelle, made with squid ink, is available from Italian delicatessens, but other colours can be used to make this dish – try a mixture of white and green.

4 Remove the scallops. Boil the wine and stock to reduce by half and add the green sauce to the pan. Heat gently to warm, then return the scallops to the pan and cook for 1 minute. Spoon over the pasta and garnish with lime wedges and parsley.

NUTRITION NOTES	
Per portion:	
Energy	368Kcals/1561kJ
Fat	4.01g
Saturated Fat	0.98g
Cholesterol	99mg
Fibre	1.91g

BAKED FISH IN BANANA LEAVES

Fish that is prepared in this way is particularly succulent and flavourful. Fillets are used here, rather than whole fish, which is easier for those who don't like to mess about with bones. It is a great dish for a barbecue.

—— INGREDIENTS ——

Serves 4

250ml/8fl oz/1 cup coconut milk
30ml/2 tbsp red curry paste
45ml/3 tbsp fish sauce
30ml/2 tbsp caster sugar
5 kaffir lime leaves, torn
4 x 175g/6oz fish fillets, such
  as snapper
175g/6oz mixed vegetables, such as
  carrots or leeks, finely shredded
4 banana leaves or pieces of foil
30ml/2 tbsp shredded spring onions, to
  garnish
2 red chillies, finely sliced, to garnish

—— NUTRITION NOTES ——

Per portion:	
Energy	258Kcals/1094kJ
Fat	4.31g
Saturated Fat	0.7g
Cholesterol	64.75mg
Fibre	1.23g

COOK'S TIP
Coconut milk is low in calories and fat and so makes an ideal basis for a low fat marinade or sauce. Choose colourful mixed vegetables such as carrots, leeks and red pepper, to make the dish more attractive and appealing.

1 Combine the coconut milk, curry paste, fish sauce, sugar and kaffir lime leaves in a shallow dish.

2 Marinate the fish in this mixture for about 15–30 minutes. Preheat the oven to 200°C/400°F/Gas 6.

3 Mix the vegetables together and lay a portion on top of a banana leaf or piece of foil. Place a piece of fish on top with a little of its marinade.

4 Wrap the fish up by turning in the sides and ends of the leaf and secure with cocktail sticks. (With foil, just crumple the edges together.) Repeat with the rest of the fish.

5 Bake for 20–25 minutes or until the fish is cooked. Alternatively, cook under the grill or on a barbecue. Just before serving, garnish the fish with a sprinkling of spring onions and sliced red chillies.

SEAFOOD SALAD WITH FRAGRANT HERBS

INGREDIENTS

Serves 6

250ml/8fl oz/1 cup fish stock or water
250g/12oz squid, cleaned and cut
    into rings
12 uncooked king prawns, shelled
12 scallops
50g/2oz bean thread noodles, soaked in
    warm water for 30 minutes
½ cucumber, cut into thin sticks
1 lemon grass stalk, finely chopped
2 kaffir lime leaves, finely shredded
2 shallots, finely sliced
juice of 1–2 limes
30ml/2 tbsp fish sauce
30ml/2 tbsp chopped spring onions
30ml/2 tbsp chopped coriander leaves
12–15 mint leaves, roughly torn
4 red chillies, seeded and sliced
coriander sprigs, to garnish

1 Pour the stock or water into a medium saucepan, set over a high heat and bring to the boil.

2 Cook each type of seafood separately in the stock. Don't overcook – it takes only a few minutes for each seafood. Remove and set aside.

3 Drain the bean thread noodles and cut them into short lengths, about 5cm/2in long. Combine the noodles with the cooked seafood.

4 Add all the remaining ingredients, mix together well and serve garnished with coriander sprigs.

NUTRITION NOTES

Per portion:	
Energy	78Kcals/332kJ
Fat	1.12g
Saturated Fat	0.26g
Cholesterol	123mg
Fibre	0.37g

COOK'S TIP
Use other prepared seafood, such as mussels and cockles, in place of the prawns or scallops. If fresh chillies are not available, use 10–15ml/2–3 tsp of hot chilli powder or, alternatively, use ready-chopped chillies.

LEMON SOLE BAKED IN A PAPER CASE

Serves 4

*4 lemon sole fillets, each weighing
   about 150g/5oz*
½ small cucumber, sliced
4 lemon slices
60ml/4 tbsp dry white wine
sprigs of fresh dill, to garnish
potatoes and braised celery, to serve

For the yogurt hollandaise
150ml/¼ pint low fat natural yogurt
5ml/1 tsp lemon juice
2 egg yolks
5ml/1 tsp Dijon mustard
salt and black pepper

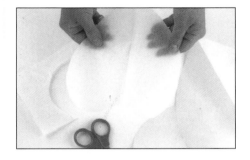

1 Preheat the oven to 180°C/350°F/
Gas 4. Cut out four heart shapes
from non-stick baking paper, each
about 20 x 15cm/8 x 6in.

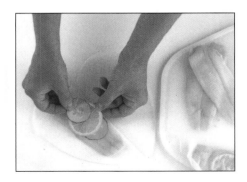

2 Place a sole fillet on one side of
each paper heart. Arrange the
cucumber and lemon slices on top of
each fillet. Sprinkle with the wine and
close the parcels by turning the edges of
the paper and twisting to secure. Put
on a baking tray and cook in the oven
for 15 minutes.

3 Meanwhile make the hollandaise.
Beat together the yogurt, lemon
juice and egg yolks in a double boiler
or bowl placed over a saucepan. Cook
over simmering water, stirring for
about 15 minutes, or until thickened.
(The sauce will become thinner after
10 minutes, but will thicken again.)

COOK'S TIP
Make sure that the paper parcels
are well sealed, so that none of
the delicious juices can escape.

4 Remove from the heat and stir in
the mustard. Season to taste with
salt and pepper. Open the fish parcels,
garnish with a sprig of dill and serve
accompanied with the sauce, new
potatoes and braised celery.

NUTRITION NOTES

Per portion:	
Energy	185Kcals/779kJ
Protein	29.27g
Fat	4.99g
Saturated Fat	1.58g
Fibre	0.27g

THAI BEEF SALAD

A hearty salad of beef, laced with a chilli and lime dressing.

INGREDIENTS

Serves 6

75g/3oz lean sirloin steaks
1 red onion, finely sliced
1/2 cucumber, finely sliced
  into matchsticks
1 lemon grass stalk, finely chopped
30ml/2 tbsp chopped spring onions
juice of 2 limes
15–30ml/1–2 tbsp fish sauce
2–4 red chillies, finely sliced, to garnish
fresh coriander, Chinese mustard cress
  and mint leaves, to garnish

NUTRITION NOTES

Per portion:

Energy	101Kcals/424kJ
Fat	3.8g
Saturated Fat	1.7g
Cholesterol	33.4mg
Fibre	0.28g

COOK'S TIP
Rump or fillet steaks would work just as well in this recipe. Choose good-quality lean steaks and remove and discard any visible fat.

1 Grill the sirloin steaks until they are medium-rare, then allow to rest for 10–15 minutes.

2 When cool, thinly slice the beef and put the slices in a large bowl.

3 Add the sliced onion, cucumber matchsticks and lemon grass.

4 Add the spring onions. Toss and season with lime juice and fish sauce. Serve at room temperature or chilled, garnished with the chillies, coriander, mustard cress and mint.

THAI-STYLE CHICKEN SALAD

This salad comes from Chiang Mai, a city in the north-east of Thailand. It's hot and spicy, and wonderfully aromatic. Choose strong-flavoured leaves, such as curly endive or rocket, for the salad.

INGREDIENTS

Serves 6
450g/1lb minced chicken breast
1 lemon grass stalk, finely chopped
3 kaffir lime leaves, finely chopped
4 red chillies, seeded and chopped
60ml/4 tbsp lime juice
30ml/2 tbsp fish sauce
15ml/1 tbsp roasted ground rice
2 spring onions, chopped
30ml/2 tbsp coriander leaves
mixed salad leaves, cucumber and
    tomato slices, to serve
mint sprigs, to garnish

1 Heat a large non-stick frying pan. Add the minced chicken and cook in a little water.

2 Stir constantly until cooked, which will take about 7–10 minutes.

3 Transfer the cooked chicken to a large bowl and add the rest of the ingredients. Mix thoroughly.

4 Serve on a bed of mixed salad leaves, cucumber and tomato slices, garnished with mint sprigs.

COOK'S TIP
Use sticky (glutinous) rice to make roasted ground rice. Put the rice in a frying pan and dry roast until golden brown. Remove and grind to a powder with a pestle and mortar or in a food processor. Keep in a glass jar in a cool dry place and use as required.

NUTRITION NOTES	
Per portion:	
Energy	106Kcals/446kJ
Fat	1.13g
Saturated Fat	0.28g
Cholesterol	52.5mg
Fibre	0.7g

FRAGRANT CHICKEN CURRY

In this dish, the mildly spiced sauce is thickened using lentils rather than the traditional onions fried in ghee.

INGREDIENTS

Serves 4–6

75g/3oz/½ cup red lentils
30ml/2 tbsp mild curry powder
10ml/2 tsp ground coriander
5ml/1 tsp cumin seeds
475ml/16fl oz/2 cups vegetable stock
8 chicken thighs, skinned
225g/8oz fresh shredded spinach, or
    frozen, thawed and well drained
15ml/1 tbsp chopped fresh coriander
salt and black pepper
sprigs of fresh coriander, to garnish
white or brown basmati rice and grilled
    poppadums, to serve

1 Rinse the lentils under cold running water. Put in a large, heavy-based saucepan with the curry powder, ground coriander, cumin seeds and stock.

2 Bring to the boil, then lower the heat. Cover and simmer gently for 10 minutes.

COOK'S TIP
Lentils are an excellent source of fibre, and add colour and texture.

3 Add the chicken and spinach. Replace the cover and simmer gently for a further 40 minutes, or until the chicken has cooked.

4 Stir in the chopped coriander and season to taste. Serve garnished with fresh coriander and accompanied by the rice and grilled poppadums.

RAGOÛT OF VEAL

If you are looking for a low-calorie dish to treat yourself – or some guests – then this is perfect, and quick, too.

INGREDIENTS

Serves 4
375g/12oz veal fillet or loin
10ml/2 tsp olive oil
10–12 tiny onions, kept whole
1 yellow pepper, seeded and cut
  into eighths
1 orange or red pepper, seeded and
  cut into eighths
3 tomatoes, peeled
  and quartered
4 fresh basil sprigs
30ml/2 tbsp dry martini or sherry
salt and black pepper

NUTRITION NOTES

Per portion:	
Energy	158Kcals/665.5kJ
Fat	4.97g
Saturated Fat	1.14g
Cholesterol	63mg
Fibre	2.5g

1 Trim off any fat and cut the veal into cubes. Heat the oil in a frying pan and gently stir-fry the veal and onions until browned.

2 After a couple of minutes, add the peppers and tomatoes. Continue stir-frying for another 4–5 minutes.

COOK'S TIP
Lean beef or pork fillet may be used instead of veal, if you prefer. Shallots can replace the onions.

3 Add half the basil leaves, roughly chopped (keep some for garnish), the martini or sherry, and seasoning. Cook, stirring frequently, for another 10 minutes, or until the meat is tender.

4 Sprinkle with the remaining basil leaves and serve hot.

VEGETABLES
& SALADS

POTATO GRATIN

The flavour of Parmesan is wonderfully strong, so a little goes a long way. Leave the cheese out altogether for an almost fat-free dish.

INGREDIENTS

Serves 4
1 garlic clove
5 large baking potatoes, peeled
*45ml/3tbsp freshly grated Parmesan
    cheese*
*600ml/1 pint/2½ cups vegetable or
    chicken stock*
pinch of grated nutmeg
salt and black pepper

1 Preheat the oven to 200°C/400°F/ Gas 6. Halve the garlic clove and rub over the base and sides of a large shallow gratin dish.

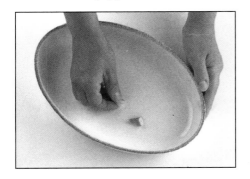

2 Slice the potatoes very thinly and arrange a third of them in the dish. Sprinkle with a little grated Parmesan cheese, and season with salt and pepper. Pour over some of the stock to prevent the potatoes from discolouring.

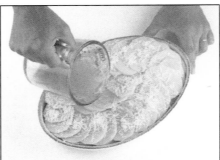

3 Continue layering the potatoes and cheese as before, then pour over the rest of the stock. Sprinkle with the grated nutmeg.

COOK'S TIP
For a potato and onion gratin, thinly slice one medium onion and layer with the potato.

4 Bake in the preheated oven for about 1¼–1½ hours or until the potatoes are tender and the tops well browned.

NUTRITION NOTES

Per portion:
Energy	178Kcals/749kJ
Protein	9.42g
Fat	1.57g
Saturated Fat	0.30g
Fibre	1.82g

Concertina Garlic Potatoes

With a low fat topping these would make a superb meal in themselves or could be enjoyed as a nutritious accompaniment to grilled fish or meat.

INGREDIENTS

Serves 4
4 baking potatoes
2 garlic cloves, cut into slivers
60ml/4 tbsp low fat fromage frais
60ml/4 tbsp low fat natural yogurt
30ml/2 tbsp snipped chives
6–8 watercress sprigs, finely chopped (optional)

NUTRITION NOTES

Per portion:
Energy	195Kcals/815kJ
Fat	3.5g
Saturated Fat	2g
Cholesterol	10mg

1 Preheat the oven to 200°C/400°F/ Gas 6. Slice each potato at about 5mm/¼in intervals, cutting not quite to the base, so that they retain their shape. Slip the slivers of the garlic between the cuts in the potatoes.

COOK'S TIP
The most suitable potatoes for baking are of the floury variety. Some of the best include Estima, Cara and Kerr's Pink.

2 Place the garlic-filled potatoes in a roasting tin and bake for 1–1¼ hours or until soft when tested with a knife. Meanwhile, mix the low fat fromage frais and yogurt in a bowl, then stir in the snipped chives, along with the watercress, if using.

3 Serve the baked potatoes on individual plates, with a dollop of the yogurt and fromage frais mixture on top of each.

Potato, Leek and Tomato Bake

INGREDIENTS

Serves 4
675g/1½lb potatoes
2 leeks, sliced
3 large tomatoes, sliced
a few fresh rosemary sprigs, crushed
1 garlic clove, crushed
300ml/½ pint/1¼ cups vegetable stock
15ml/1 tbsp olive oil
salt and black pepper

NUTRITION NOTES

Per portion:
Energy	180Kcals/740kJ
Fat	3.5g
Saturated Fat	0.5g
Cholesterol	0

1 Preheat the oven to 180°C/350°F/ Gas 4 and grease a 1.2 litre/ 2 pint/5 cup shallow ovenproof dish. Scrub and thinly slice the potatoes. Layer them with the leeks and tomatoes in the dish, scattering some rosemary between the layers and ending with a layer of potatoes.

2 Add the garlic to the stock, stir in salt if needed and pepper to taste, then pour over the vegetables. Brush the top layer of potatoes with olive oil.

3 Bake for 1¼–1½ hours until the potatoes are tender and the topping is golden and slightly crisp.

COURGETTES IN CITRUS SAUCE

If baby courgettes are unavailable, you can use larger ones, but they should be cooked whole so that they don't absorb too much water. After cooking, halve them lengthways and cut into 10cm/4in lengths. These tender, baby courgettes served in a very low fat sauce make this a tasty and low fat accompaniment to grilled fish fillets.

NUTRITION NOTES

Per portion:

Energy	33Kcals/138kJ
Protein	2.18g
Fat	0.42g
Saturated Fat	0.09g
Fibre	0.92g

INGREDIENTS

Serves 4

350g/12oz baby courgettes
4 spring onions, finely sliced
2.5cm/1in fresh root ginger, grated
30ml/2 tbsp cider vinegar
15ml/1 tbsp light soy sauce
5ml/1 tsp soft light brown sugar
45ml/3 tbsp vegetable stock
finely grated rind and juice of ½ lemon
  and ½ orange
5ml/1 tsp cornflour

1 Cook the courgettes in lightly salted boiling water for 3–4 minutes, or until just tender. Drain well.

2 Meanwhile, put all the remaining ingredients, except the cornflour, into a small saucepan and bring to the boil. Simmer for 3 minutes.

3 Blend the cornflour with 10ml/2 tsp cold water and add to the sauce. Bring to the boil, stirring continuously, until the sauce has thickened.

4 Pour the sauce over the courgettes and heat gently, shaking the pan to coat them evenly. Transfer to a warmed serving dish and serve.

COOK'S TIP
Use baby sweetcorn or aubergines in place of the courgettes for an appetizing change.

ROASTED MEDITERRANEAN VEGETABLES

For a really colourful dish, try these vegetables roasted in olive oil with garlic and rosemary. The flavour is wonderfully intense.

INGREDIENTS

Serves 6
1 each red and yellow pepper
2 Spanish onions
2 large courgettes
1 large aubergine or 4 baby aubergines, trimmed
1 fennel bulb, thickly sliced
2 beef tomatoes
8 fat garlic cloves
30ml/2 tbsp olive oil
fresh rosemary sprigs
black pepper
lemon wedges and black olives (optional), to garnish

1 Halve and seed the peppers, then cut them into large chunks. Peel the onions and cut into thick wedges.

NUTRITION NOTES

Per portion:	
Energy	120Kcals/504kJ
Fat	5.2g
Saturated Fat	0.68g
Cholesterol	0

2 Cut the courgettes and aubergines into large chunks.

3 Preheat the oven to 220°C/425°F/ Gas 7. Spread the peppers, onions, courgettes, aubergines and fennel in a lightly oiled, shallow ovenproof dish or roasting pan, or, if liked, arrange in rows to make a colourful design.

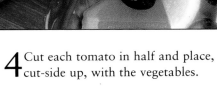

4 Cut each tomato in half and place, cut-side up, with the vegetables.

5 Tuck the garlic cloves among the vegetables, then brush them with the olive oil. Place some sprigs of rosemary among the vegetables and grind over some black pepper, particularly on the tomatoes.

6 Roast for 20–25 minutes, turning the vegetables halfway through the cooking time. Serve from the dish or on a flat platter, garnished with lemon wedges. Scatter some black olives over the top, if you like.

VEGETABLES À LA GRECQUE

This simple side salad is made with winter vegetables, but you can vary it according to the season. This combination of vegetables makes an ideal, low fat side salad to serve with grilled lean meat or poultry, or with thick slices of fresh, crusty bread.

INGREDIENTS

Serves 4

175ml/6fl oz/¾ cup white wine
5ml/1 tsp olive oil
30ml/2 tbsp lemon juice
2 bay leaves
sprig of fresh thyme
4 juniper berries
450g/1lb leeks, trimmed and cut into
  2.5cm/1in lengths
1 small cauliflower, broken into florets
4 celery sticks, sliced on the diagonal
30ml/2 tbsp chopped fresh parsley
salt and black pepper

1 Put the wine, oil, lemon juice, bay leaves, thyme and juniper berries into a large, heavy-based saucepan and bring to the boil. Cover and let simmer for 20 minutes.

NUTRITION NOTES

Per portion:

Energy	88Kcals/368kJ
Protein	4.53g
Fat	2.05g
Saturated Fat	0.11g
Fibre	4.42g

2 Add the leeks, cauliflower and celery. Simmer very gently for 5–6 minutes or until just tender.

3 Remove the vegetables with a slotted spoon and transfer them to a serving dish. Briskly boil the cooking liquid for 15–20 minutes, or until reduced by half. Strain.

4 Stir the parsley into the liquid and season with salt and pepper to taste. Pour over the vegetables and leave to cool. Chill in the fridge for at least 1 hour before serving.

COOK'S TIP
Choose a dry or medium-dry white wine for best results.

GREEN PAPAYA SALAD

There are many variations of this salad in south-east Asia. As green papaya is not easy to get hold of, shredded carrots, cucumber or green apple may be substituted. Serve this salad with raw white cabbage and rice.

INGREDIENTS

Serves 4
1 medium green papaya
4 garlic cloves
15ml/1 tbsp chopped shallots
3–4 red chillies, seeded and sliced
2.5ml/¹/₂ tsp salt
2–3 French or runner beans, cut into
  2cm/³/₄in lengths
2 tomatoes, cut into wedges
45ml/3 tbsp fish sauce
15ml/1 tbsp caster sugar
juice of 1 lime
30ml/2 tbsp crushed roasted peanuts
sliced red chillies, to garnish

1 Peel the papaya and cut in half lengthways, scrape out the seeds with a spoon and finely shred the flesh.

2 Grind the garlic, shallots, chillies and salt together in a large mortar with a pestle.

NUTRITION NOTES

Per portion:
Energy	96Kcals/402kJ
Fat	4.2g
Saturated Fat	0.77g
Cholesterol	0

3 Add the shredded papaya a little at a time and pound until it becomes slightly limp and soft.

4 Add the sliced beans and tomatoes and lightly crush. Season with fish sauce, sugar and lime juice.

5 Transfer the salad to a serving dish, sprinkle with crushed peanuts and garnish with chillies.

COOK'S TIP
If you do not have a large pestle and mortar, use a bowl and crush the shredded papaya with a wooden meat tenderizer or the end of a rolling pin.

AUBERGINE SALAD

An appetizing and unusual salad that you will find yourself making over and over again.

INGREDIENTS

Serves 6
2 aubergines
15ml/1 tbsp oil
30ml/2 tbsp dried shrimps, soaked
  and drained
15ml/1 tbsp coarsely chopped garlic
30ml/2 tbsp freshly squeezed lime juice
5ml/1 tsp palm sugar
30ml/2 tbsp fish sauce
1 hard-boiled egg, chopped
4 shallots, thinly sliced into rings
coriander leaves, to garnish
2 red chillies, seeded and sliced,
  to garnish

COOK'S TIP
For an interesting variation, try using salted duck's or quail's eggs, cut in half, instead of chopped hen's eggs.

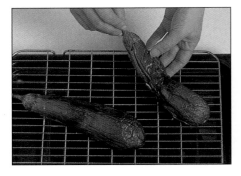

1 Grill or roast the aubergines until charred and tender.

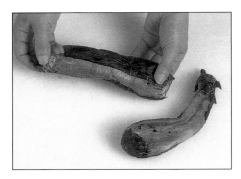

2 When cool enough to handle, peel away the skin and slice the aubergine into thick pieces.

3 Heat the oil in a small frying pan, add the drained shrimps and the garlic and fry until golden. Remove from the pan and set aside.

4 To make the dressing, put the lime juice, palm sugar and fish sauce in a small bowl and whisk together.

5 To serve, arrange the aubergine on a serving dish. Top with the chopped egg, shallot rings and dried shrimp mixture. Drizzle over the dressing and garnish with coriander and red chillies.

NUTRITION NOTES	
Per portion:	
Energy	70.5Kcals/295kJ
Fat	3.76g
Saturated Fat	0.68g
Cholesterol	57mg
Fibre	1.20g

BAMBOO SHOOT SALAD

This salad, which has a hot and sharp flavour, originated in north-east Thailand. Use fresh young bamboo shoots if you can find them, otherwise substitute canned bamboo shoots.

INGREDIENTS

Serves 4

400g/14oz can whole bamboo shoots
25g/1oz glutinous rice
30ml/2 tbsp chopped shallots
15ml/1 tbsp chopped garlic
45ml/3 tbsp chopped spring onions
30ml/2 tbsp fish sauce
30ml/2 tbsp lime juice
5ml/1 tsp granulated sugar
2.5ml/¹/₂ tsp dried flaked chillies
20–25 small mint leaves
15ml/1 tbsp toasted sesame seeds

1 Rinse and drain the bamboo shoots, then slice and set aside.

2 Dry roast the rice in a frying pan until it is golden brown. Remove and grind to fine crumbs with a pestle and mortar.

3 Tip the rice into a bowl, add the shallots, garlic, spring onions, fish sauce, lime juice, granulated sugar, chillies and half the mint leaves.

COOK'S TIP
Omit the sesame seeds to reduce calories and fat. Use ready-minced or "lazy" garlic instead of crushing your own.

4 Mix thoroughly, then pour over the bamboo shoots and toss together. Serve sprinkled with sesame seeds and the remaining mint leaves.

NUTRITION NOTES	
Per portion:	
Energy	73.5Kcals/308kJ
Fat	2.8g
Saturated Fat	0.41g
Cholesterol	0
Fibre	2.45g

FRUIT AND FIBRE SALAD

Fresh, fast and filling, this salad makes a great supper or snack.

INGREDIENTS

Serves 6

225g/8oz red or white cabbage, or a
　mixture of both
3 medium carrots
1 pear
1 red-skinned eating apple
200g/7oz can green flageolet beans,
　drained
50g/2oz/¼ cup chopped dates

For the dressing

2.5ml/½ tsp dry English mustard
10ml/2 tsp clear honey
30ml/2 tbsp orange juice
5ml/1 tsp white wine vinegar
2.5ml/½ tsp paprika
salt and black pepper

1 Shred the cabbage very finely, discarding the core and tough ribs.

2 Cut the carrots into very thin strips, about 5cm/2in long.

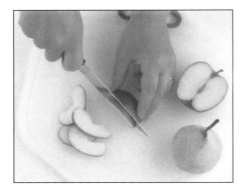

3 Quarter, core and slice the pear and the apple, leaving the peel on.

4 Put the fruit and vegetables in a bowl with the beans and dates. Mix well.

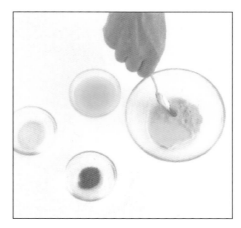

5 To make the dressing, blend the mustard with the honey until smooth. Add the orange juice, vinegar, paprika and seasoning and mix well.

6 Pour the dressing over the salad and toss to coat. Chill in the fridge for 30 minutes before serving.

NUTRITION NOTES

Per portion:

Energy	137Kcals/574kJ
Fat	0.87g
Saturated Fat	0.03g
Fibre	6.28g

COOK'S TIP

Use other canned beans, such as red kidney beans or chick-peas, in place of the flageolet beans. Add 2.5ml/½ tsp ground spice, such as chilli powder, cumin or coriander, for extra flavour. Add 5ml/1 tsp finely grated orange or lemon rind to the dressing, for extra flavour.

BULGUR WHEAT SALAD WITH ORANGES

Bulgur wheat makes an excellent alternative to rice or pasta.

INGREDIENTS

Serves 6
1 small green pepper
150g/5oz/1 cup bulgur wheat
600ml/1 pint/2½ cups water
½ cucumber, diced
15g/½oz/½ cup chopped fresh mint
40g/1½oz/⅓ cup flaked almonds, toasted
grated rind and juice of 1 lemon
2 seedless oranges
salt and black pepper
mint sprigs, to garnish

1 Using a sharp vegetable knife, carefully halve and seed the green pepper. Cut it on a board into small cubes and put to one side.

2 Place the bulgur wheat in a saucepan and add the water. Bring to the boil, lower the heat, cover and simmer for 10–15 minutes until tender. Alternatively, place the bulgur wheat in a heatproof bowl, pour over boiling water and leave to soak for 30 minutes. Most, if not all, of the water should be absorbed; drain off any excess.

3 Toss the bulgur wheat with the cucumber, green pepper, mint and toasted almonds in a serving bowl. Add the grated lemon rind and juice.

4 Cut the rind from the oranges, then working over the bowl to catch the juice, cut the oranges into neat segments. Add to the bulgur mixture, then season and toss lightly. Garnish with the mint sprigs.

NUTRITION NOTES	
Per portion:	
Energy	160Kcals/672kJ
Fat	4.3g
Saturated Fat	0.33g
Cholesterol	0

BROWN RICE SALAD WITH FRUIT

An Oriental-style dressing gives this colourful rice salad extra piquancy. Whole grains like brown rice are unrefined, so they retain their natural fibre, vitamins and minerals.

INGREDIENTS

Serves 4–6
115g/4oz/⅔ cup brown rice
1 small red pepper, seeded and diced
200g/7oz can sweetcorn niblets,
  drained
45ml/3 tbsp sultanas
225g/8oz can pineapple pieces in
  fruit juice
15ml/1 tbsp light soy sauce
5ml/1 tsp sunflower oil
10ml/2 tsp hazelnut oil
1 garlic clove, crushed
5ml/1 tsp finely chopped fresh
  root ginger
ground black pepper
4 spring onions, sliced, to garnish

COOK'S TIP
Hazelnut oil, which contains mainly monounsaturated fats, adds a wonderful flavour.

1 Cook the brown rice in a large saucepan of lightly salted boiling water for about 30 minutes, or until it is tender. Drain thoroughly and cool. Meanwhile, prepare the garnish by slicing the spring onions at an angle and setting aside.

2 Tip the rice into a bowl and add the red pepper, sweetcorn and sultanas. Drain the pineapple pieces, reserving the juice, add them to the rice mixture and toss lightly.

3 Pour the reserved pineapple juice into a clean screw-top jar. Add the soy sauce, sunflower and hazelnut oils, garlic and root ginger. Add some salt and pepper, then close the jar tightly and shake well to combine.

4 Pour the dressing over the salad and toss well. Scatter the spring onions over the top.

NUTRITION NOTES	
Per portion:	
Energy	245Kcals/1029kJ
Fat	4.25g
Saturated Fat	0.6g
Cholesterol	0

CRAB PASTA SALAD

Low fat yogurt makes a piquant dressing for this salad.

INGREDIENTS

Serves 6

350g/12oz pasta twists
1 small red pepper, seeded and
   finely chopped
2 x 175g/6oz cans white crab
   meat, drained
115g/4oz cherry tomatoes, halved
1/4 cucumber, halved, seeded and sliced
   into crescents
15ml/1 tbsp lemon juice
300ml/1/2 pint/1 1/4 cups low fat yogurt
2 celery sticks, finely chopped
10ml/2 tsp horseradish cream
2.5ml/1/2 tsp paprika
2.5ml/1/2 tsp Dijon mustard
30ml/2 tbsp sweet tomato pickle
   or chutney
salt and black pepper
fresh basil, to garnish

1 Cook the pasta in a large pan of boiling, salted water, according to the instructions on the packet, until *al dente*. Drain and rinse thoroughly under cold water.

2 Cover the chopped red pepper with boiling water and leave to stand for 1 minute. Drain and rinse under cold water. Pat dry on kitchen paper.

NUTRITION NOTES

Per portion:	
Energy	305Kcals/1283kJ
Fat	2.5g
Saturated Fat	0.5g
Cholesterol	43mg
Fibre	2.9g

3 Drain the crab meat and pick over carefully for pieces of shell. Put into a bowl with the halved tomatoes and sliced cucumber. Season with salt and pepper and sprinkle with lemon juice.

4 To make the dressing, add the red pepper to the yogurt, with the celery, horseradish cream, paprika, mustard and sweet tomato pickle or chutney. Mix the pasta with the dressing and transfer to a serving dish. Spoon the crab mixture on top and garnish with fresh basil.

CACHUMBAR

Cachumbar is a salad relish most commonly served with Indian curries. There are many versions; this one will leave your mouth feeling cool and fresh after a spicy meal.

INGREDIENTS

Serves 4
3 ripe tomatoes
2 chopped spring onions
1.5ml/¼ tsp caster sugar
salt
45ml/3 tbsp chopped fresh coriander

NUTRITION NOTES

Per portion:	
Energy	9.5Kcals/73.5kJ
Fat	0.23g
Saturated Fat	0.07g
Cholesterol	0
Fibre	0.87g

1 Remove the tough cores from the bottom of the tomatoes with a small sharp-pointed knife.

COOK'S TIP
Cachumbar also makes a fine accompaniment to fresh crab, lobster and shellfish.

2 Halve the tomatoes, remove the seeds and dice the flesh.

3 Combine the tomatoes with the spring onions, sugar, salt and chopped coriander. Serve at room temperature.

DESSERTS

FILO CHIFFON PIE

Filo pastry is low in fat and is very easy to use. Keep a pack in the freezer, ready to make impressive desserts like this one.

Serves 6
500g/1¼lb rhubarb
5ml/1 tsp mixed spice
finely grated rind and juice of 1 orange
15ml/1 tbsp granulated sugar
15g/½oz/1 tbsp butter
3 filo pastry sheets

1 Preheat the oven to 200°C/400°F/ Gas 6. Chop the rhubarb into 2.5cm/1in pieces and put them in a bowl.

2 Add the mixed spice, orange rind and juice and sugar. Tip the rhubarb into a 1 litre/1¾ pint/4 cup pie dish.

NUTRITION NOTES	
Per portion:	
Energy	71Kcals/299kJ
Fat	2.5g
Saturated Fat	1.41g
Cholesterol	5.74mg
Fibre	1.48g

3 Melt the butter and brush it over the pastry. Lift the pastry on to the pie dish, butter-side up, and crumple it up decoratively to cover the pie.

VARIATION
Other fruit can be used in this pie – just prepare depending on type.

4 Put the dish on a baking sheet and bake for 20 minutes, until golden brown. Reduce the heat to 180°C/350°F/ Gas 4 and bake for a further 10–15 minutes, until the rhubarb is tender.

BLUSHING PEARS

Pears poached in rosé wine and sweet spices absorb all the subtle flavours and turn a delightful soft pink colour.

INGREDIENTS

Serves 6
6 *firm eating pears*
300ml/½ pint/1¼ cups rosé wine
150ml/¼ pint/⅔ cup cranberry or
clear apple juice
strip of thinly pared orange rind
1 cinnamon stick
4 whole cloves
1 bay leaf
75ml/5 tbsp caster sugar
small bay leaves, to decorate

1 Thinly peel the pears with a sharp knife or vegetable peeler, leaving the stalks attached.

2 Pour the wine and cranberry or apple juice into a large heavy-based saucepan. Add the orange rind, cinnamon stick, cloves, bay leaf and sugar.

3 Heat gently, stirring all the time, until the sugar has dissolved. Add the pears and stand them upright in the pan. Pour in enough cold water to barely cover them. Cover and cook gently for 20–30 minutes, or until just tender, turning and basting occasionally.

4 Using a slotted spoon, gently lift the pears out of the syrup and transfer to a serving dish.

5 Bring the syrup to the boil and boil rapidly for 10–15 minutes, or until it has reduced by half.

6 Strain the syrup and pour over the pears. Serve hot or well-chilled, decorated with small bay leaves.

NUTRITION NOTES

Per portion:
Energy	148Kcals/620kJ
Fat	0.16g
Saturated Fat	0
Fibre	2.93g

COOK'S TIP
Check the pears by piercing with a skewer or sharp knife towards the end of the poaching time, because some may cook more quickly than others. Serve straight away, or leave to cool in the syrup and then chill.

Baked Apples in Honey and Lemon

A classic mix of flavours in a healthy, traditional family pudding. Serve warm, with skimmed-milk custard or low fat frozen yogurt.

NUTRITION NOTES

Per portion:
Energy	61Kcals/259.5kJ
Fat	1.62g
Saturated Fat	0.42g
Cholesterol	0.25mg

INGREDIENTS

Serves 4
4 medium cooking apples
15ml/1 tbsp clear honey
grated rind and juice of 1 lemon
15ml/1 tbsp low fat spread
skimmed-milk custard, to serve

1 Preheat the oven to 180°C/350°F/ Gas 4. Remove the cores from the apples, leaving them whole.

2 With a cannelle or sharp knife, cut lines through the apple skin at intervals. Put the apples in an oven-proof dish.

3 Mix together the honey, lemon rind, juice and low fat spread.

4 Spoon the mixture into the apples and cover the dish with foil or a lid. Bake for 40–45 minutes, or until the apples are tender. Serve with skimmed-milk custard.

APPLE AND BLACKCURRANT PANCAKES

These pancakes are made with a wholewheat batter and are filled with a delicious fruit mixture.

INGREDIENTS

Makes 10

115g/4oz/1 cup plain wholemeal flour
300ml/½ pint/1¼ cups skimmed milk
1 egg, beaten
15ml/1 tbsp sunflower oil, plus extra
  for greasing
half fat crème fraîche, to serve
  (optional)
toasted nuts or sesame seeds, for
  sprinkling (optional)

For the filling

450g/1lb cooking apples
225g/8oz blackcurrants
30–45ml/2–3 tbsp water
30ml/2 tbsp demerara sugar

1 To make the pancake batter, put the flour in a mixing bowl and make a well in the centre.

2 Add a little of the milk with the egg and the oil. Beat the flour into the liquid, then gradually beat in the rest of the milk, keeping the batter smooth and free from lumps. Cover the batter and chill while you prepare the filling.

COOK'S TIP
If you wish, substitute other combinations of fruit for apples and blackcurrants.

3 Quarter, peel and core the apples. Slice them into a pan and add the blackcurrants and water. Cook over a gentle heat for 10–15 minutes until the fruit is soft. Stir in enough demerara sugar to sweeten.

NUTRITION NOTES

Per portion:

Energy	120Kcals/505kJ
Fat	3g
Saturated Fat	0.5g
Cholesterol	25mg

4 Lightly grease a non-stick pan with just a smear of oil. Heat the pan, pour in about 30ml/2 tbsp of the batter, swirl it around and cook for about 1 minute. Flip the pancake over with a palette knife and cook the other side. Put on a sheet of kitchen paper and keep hot while cooking the remaining pancakes.

5 Fill the pancakes with the apple and blackcurrant mixture and roll them up. Serve with a dollop of crème fraîche, if using, and sprinkle with nuts or sesame seeds, if liked.

RASPBERRY VACHERIN

Meringue rounds filled with orange-flavoured low fat fromage frais and fresh raspberries make this a perfect dinner party dessert.

INGREDIENTS

Serves 6
3 egg whites
175g/6oz/³⁄4 cup caster sugar
5ml/1 tsp chopped almonds
icing sugar, for dusting
raspberry leaves, to decorate (optional)

For the filling
175g/6oz/³⁄4 cup low fat soft cheese
15–30ml/1–2 tbsp clear honey
15–30ml/1–2 tbsp Cointreau
120ml/4fl oz/¹⁄2 cup low fat
* fromage frais*
225g/8oz raspberries

NUTRITION NOTES

Per portion:	
Energy	197Kcals/837.5kJ
Fat	1.02g
Saturated Fat	0.36g
Cholesterol	1.67mg
Fibre	1g

COOK'S TIP
When making the meringue, whisk the egg whites until they are so stiff that you can turn the bowl upside-down without them falling out.

1 Preheat the oven to 140°C/275°F/ Gas 1. Draw a 20cm/8in circle on two pieces of non-stick baking paper. Turn the paper over so the marking is on the underside and use it to line two heavy baking sheets.

2 Whisk the egg whites in a clean bowl until very stiff, then gradually whisk in the caster sugar to make a stiff meringue mixture.

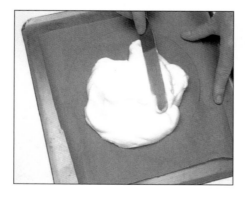

3 Spoon the mixture on to the circles on the prepared baking sheets, spreading the meringue evenly to the edges. Sprinkle one meringue round with the chopped almonds.

4 Bake for 1¹⁄2–2 hours until crisp and dry, and then carefully lift the meringue rounds off the baking sheets. Peel away the paper and cool the meringues on a wire rack.

5 To make the filling, cream the soft cheese with the honey and liqueur in a bowl. Gradually fold in the fromage frais and the raspberries, reserving three berries for decoration.

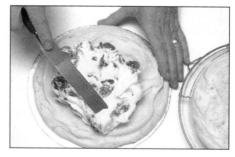

6 Place the plain meringue round on a board, spread with the filling and top with the nut-covered round. Dust with the icing sugar, transfer to a serving plate and decorate with the reserved raspberries and a sprig of raspberry leaves, if you like.

COOL GREEN FRUIT SALAD

A sophisticated, simple fruit salad for any time of year.

INGREDIENTS

Serves 6
3 Ogen or Galia melons
115g/4oz green seedless grapes
2 kiwi fruit
1 star fruit
1 green-skinned eating apple
1 lime
175ml/6fl oz/¾ cup sparkling grape juice

NUTRITION NOTES

Per portion:
Energy	67Kcals/285kJ
Fat	0.27g
Saturated Fat	0
Cholesterol	0
Fibre	1.22g

1 Cut the melons in half and scoop out the seeds. Keeping the shells intact, scoop out the fruit with a melon baller, or scoop it out with a spoon and cut into bite-size cubes. Set aside the melon shells.

COOK'S TIP
If you're serving this dessert on a hot summer day, serve the filled melon shells nestling on a platter of crushed ice to keep them beautifully cool.

2 Remove any stems from the grapes, and, if they are large, cut them in half. Peel and chop the kiwi fruit. Thinly slice the star fruit. Core and thinly slice the apple and place the slices in a bowl, with the melon, grapes, kiwi fruit and star fruit.

3 Thinly pare the rind from the lime and cut it into fine strips. Blanch the strips in boiling water for 30 seconds, then drain them and rinse in cold water. Squeeze the juice from the lime and toss it into the fruit. Mix gently.

4 Spoon the prepared fruit into the melon shells and chill in the fridge until required. Just before serving, spoon the sparkling grape juice over the fruit and scatter it with the blanched lime rind.

ICED ORANGES

The ultimate fat-free treat – these delectable orange sorbets served in fruit shells were originally sold in the beach cafés in the south of France.

--- INGREDIENTS ---

Serves 8
150g/5oz/⅔ cup granulated sugar
juice of 1 lemon
14 medium oranges
8 fresh bay leaves, to decorate

--- NUTRITION NOTES ---

Per portion:

Energy	139Kcals/593kJ
Fat	0.17g
Saturated Fat	0
Cholesterol	0
Fibre	3g

COOK'S TIP
Use crumpled kitchen paper to keep the shells upright.

1 Put the sugar in a heavy-based saucepan. Add half the lemon juice, then add 120ml/4fl oz/½ cup water. Cook over a low heat until the sugar has dissolved. Bring to the boil and boil for 2–3 minutes until the syrup is clear.

2 Slice the tops off eight of the oranges to make "hats". Scoop out the flesh of the oranges and reserve. Freeze the empty orange shells and "hats" until needed.

3 Grate the rind of the remaining oranges and add to the syrup. Squeeze the juice from the oranges, and from the reserved flesh. There should be 750ml/1¼ pints/3 cups. Squeeze another orange or add bought orange juice, if necessary.

4 Stir the orange juice and remaining lemon juice, with 90ml/6 tbsp water into the syrup. Taste, adding more lemon juice or sugar as desired. Pour the mixture into a shallow freezer container and freeze for 3 hours.

5 Turn the orange sorbet mixture into a bowl and whisk thoroughly to break up the ice crystals. Freeze for 4 hours more, until firm, but not solid.

6 Pack the mixture into the hollowed-out orange shells, mounding it up, and set the "hats" on top. Freeze the sorbet shells until ready to serve. Just before serving, push a skewer into the tops of the "hats" and push in a bay leaf, to decorate.

Yogurt Sundaes with Passion Fruit

Here is a sundae you can enjoy every day! The frozen yogurt has less fat and fewer calories than traditional ice cream, and the fruits provide vitamins A and C.

INGREDIENTS

Serves 4

350g/12oz strawberries, hulled
  and halved
2 passion fruit, halved
10ml/2 tsp icing sugar (optional)
2 ripe peaches, stoned and chopped
8 scoops (about 350g/12oz) vanilla or
  strawberry frozen yogurt

COOK'S TIP
Choose reduced fat or virtually
fat free frozen yogurt or ice
cream, to cut the calories and fat.

1 Puree half the strawberries. Scoop out the passion fruit pulp and add it to the coulis. Sweeten, if necessary.

NUTRITION NOTES

Per portion:

Energy	135Kcals/560kJ
Fat	1g
Saturated Fat	0.5g
Cholesterol	3.5mg

2 Spoon half the remaining strawberries and half the chopped peaches into four tall sundae glasses. Top each dessert with a scoop of frozen yogurt. Set aside a few choice pieces of fruit for decoration, and use the rest to make a further layer on the top of each sundae. Top each sundae with a final scoop of frozen yogurt.

3 Pour over the passion fruit coulis and decorate the sundaes with the remaining strawberries and pieces of peach. Serve immediately.

Fruit Fondue with Hazelnut Dip

INGREDIENTS

Serves 2

selection of fresh fruit for dipping, such
  as satsumas, kiwi fruit, grapes
  and physalis (cape gooseberries)
50g/2oz/½ cup reduced fat soft cheese
150ml/5fl oz/1¼ cup low fat
  hazelnut yogurt
5ml/1 tsp vanilla essence
5ml/1 tsp caster sugar

NUTRITION NOTES

Per portion (dip only):

Energy	170Kcals/714kJ
Fat	4g
Saturated Fat	2.5g
Cholesterol	6.5mg

1 First prepare the fruit. Peel and segment the satsumas, removing as much of the white pith as possible. Quarter the kiwi fruits, wash the grapes and peel back the papery casing on the physalis.

2 Beat the soft cheese with the yogurt, vanilla essence and sugar in a bowl. Spoon the mixture into a glass serving dish set on a platter or into small pots on individual plates.

3 Arrange the prepared fruits around the dip and serve immediately.

CAKES,
BAKES &
COOKIES

ANGEL CAKE

A delicious light cake to serve as a dessert for a special occasion.

INGREDIENTS

Serves 10
40g/1¹/₂oz/¹/₃ cup cornflour
40g/1¹/₂oz/¹/₃ cup plain flour
8 egg whites
225g/8oz/1 cup caster sugar, plus extra for sprinkling
5ml/1 tsp vanilla essence
90ml/6 tbsp orange-flavoured glacé icing, 4–6 physalis and a little icing sugar, to decorate

1 Preheat the oven to 180°C/350°F/ Gas 4. Sift both flours on to a sheet of greaseproof paper.

2 Whisk the egg whites in a large, clean, dry bowl until very stiff, then gradually add the sugar and vanilla essence, whisking until the mixture is thick and glossy.

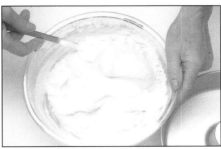

3 Gently fold in the flour mixture with a large metal spoon. Spoon into an ungreased 25cm/10in angel cake tin, smooth the surface and bake for about 45–50 minutes, until the cake springs back when lightly pressed.

COOK'S TIP
If you prefer, omit the glacé icing and physalis and simply dust the cake with a little icing sugar – it is delicious to serve as a coffee-time treat, and also makes the perfect accompaniment to vanilla yogurt ice cream for a dessert.

4 Sprinkle a piece of greaseproof paper with caster sugar and set an egg cup in the centre. Invert the cake tin over the paper, balancing it carefully on the egg cup. When cold, the cake will drop out of the tin. Transfer it to a plate, spoon over the glacé icing, arrange the physalis on top and then dust with icing sugar and serve.

NUTRITION NOTES
Per portion:

Energy	139Kcals/582kJ
Fat	0.08g
Saturated Fat	0.01g
Cholesterol	0
Fibre	0.13g

TIA MARIA GÂTEAU

A feather-light coffee sponge with a creamy liqueur-flavoured filling.

INGREDIENTS

Serves 8
75g/3oz/¾ cup plain flour
30ml/2 tbsp instant coffee powder
3 eggs
115g/4oz/½ cup caster sugar
coffee beans, to decorate (optional)

For the filling
175g/6oz/¾ cup low fat soft cheese
15ml/1 tbsp clear honey
15ml/1 tbsp Tia Maria liqueur
50g/2oz/¼ cup stem ginger,
* roughly chopped*

For the icing
225g/8oz/1¾ cups icing sugar, sifted
10ml/2 tsp coffee essence
15ml/1 tbsp water
5ml/1 tsp reduced fat cocoa powder

NUTRITION NOTES

Per portion:

Energy	226Kcals/951kJ
Fat	3.14g
Saturated Fat	1.17g
Cholesterol	75.03mg
Fibre	0.64g

COOK'S TIP
When folding in the flour mixture in step 3, be careful not to remove the air, as it helps the cake to rise.

1 Preheat the oven to 190°C/375°F/ Gas 5. Grease and line a 20cm/8in deep round cake tin. Sift the flour and coffee powder together on to a sheet of greaseproof paper.

2 Whisk the eggs and sugar in a bowl with a hand-held electric whisk until thick and mousse-like. (When the whisk is lifted, a trail should remain on the surface of the mixture for at least 15 seconds.)

3 Gently fold in the flour mixture with a metal spoon. Turn the mixture into the prepared tin. Bake the sponge for 30–35 minutes or until it springs back when lightly pressed. Turn on to a wire rack to cool completely.

4 To make the filling, mix the soft cheese with the honey in a bowl. Beat until smooth, then stir in the Tia Maria and chopped stem ginger.

5 Split the cake in half horizontally and sandwich the two halves together with the Tia Maria filling.

6 Make the icing. In a bowl, mix the icing sugar and coffee essence with enough water to make a consistency that will coat the back of a wooden spoon. Pour three-quarters of the icing over the cake, spreading it evenly to the edges. Stir the cocoa into the remaining icing until smooth. Spoon into a piping bag fitted with a writing nozzle and pipe the mocha icing over the coffee icing. Decorate with coffee beans, if liked.

RASPBERRY MUFFINS

These American muffins are made using baking powder and low fat buttermilk, giving them a light and spongy texture. They are delicious to eat at any time of the day.

INGREDIENTS

Makes 10–12
275g/10oz/2½ cups plain flour
15ml/1 tbsp baking powder
115g/4oz/½ cup caster sugar
1 egg
250ml/8fl oz/1 cup buttermilk
60ml/4 tbsp sunflower oil
150g/5oz raspberries

1 Preheat the oven to 200°C/400°F/ Gas 6. Arrange 12 paper cake cases in a deep muffin tin. Sift the flour and baking powder into a mixing bowl, stir in the sugar, then make a well in the centre.

NUTRITION NOTES

Per muffin:
Energy	171Kcals/719kJ
Fat	4.55g
Saturated Fat	0.71g
Cholesterol	16.5mg
Fibre	1.02g

2 Mix the egg, buttermilk and sun- flower oil together in a bowl, pour into the flour mixture and mix quickly.

3 Add the raspberries and lightly fold in with a metal spoon. Spoon the mixture into the paper cases.

4 Bake the muffins for 20–25 minutes until golden brown and firm in the middle. Transfer to a wire rack and serve warm or cold.

DATE AND APPLE MUFFINS

You will only need one or two of these wholesome muffins per person, as they are very filling.

INGREDIENTS

Makes 12
150g/5oz/1¼ cups self-raising
  wholemeal flour
150g/5oz/1¼ cups self-raising
  white flour
5ml/1 tsp ground cinnamon
5ml/1 tsp baking powder
25g/1 oz/2 tbsp soft margarine
75g/3oz/½ cup light muscovado sugar
1 eating apple
250ml/8fl oz/1 cup apple juice
30ml/2 tbsp pear and apple spread
1 egg, lightly beaten
75g/3oz/½ cup chopped dates
15ml/1 tbsp chopped pecan nuts

1 Preheat the oven to 200°C/400°F/ Gas 6. Arrange 12 paper cake cases in a deep muffin tin. Put the wholemeal flour in a mixing bowl. Sift in the white flour with the cinnamon and baking powder. Rub in the margarine until the mixture resembles breadcrumbs, then stir in the muscovado sugar.

NUTRITION NOTES

Per muffin:
Energy	163Kcals/686kJ
Fat	2.98g
Saturated Fat	0.47g
Cholesterol	16.04mg
Fibre	1.97g

2 Quarter and core the apple, chop the flesh finely and set aside. Stir a little of the apple juice with the pear and apple spread until smooth. Mix in the remaining juice, then add to the rubbed-in mixture with the egg. Add the chopped apple to the bowl with the dates. Mix quickly until just combined.

COOK'S TIP
Use a pear in place of the eating apple and chopped ready-to-eat dried apricots in place of the dates. Ground mixed spice is a good alternative to cinnamon.

3 Divide the mixture among the muffin cases.

4 Sprinkle with the chopped pecan nuts. Bake the muffins for 20–25 minutes until golden brown and firm in the middle. Remove to a wire rack and serve while still warm.

CINNAMON APPLE GÂTEAU

Make this lovely cake for an autumn celebration.

INGREDIENTS

Serves 8
3 eggs
115g/4oz/½ cup caster sugar
75g/3oz/¾ cup plain flour
5ml/1 tsp ground cinnamon

For the filling and topping
4 large eating apples
60ml/4 tbsp clear honey
15ml/1 tbsp water
75g/3oz/½ cup sultanas
2.5ml/½ tsp ground cinnamon
350g/12oz/1½ cups low fat soft cheese
60ml/4 tbsp reduced fat fromage frais
10ml/2 tsp lemon juice
45ml/3 tbsp apricot glaze
mint sprig, to decorate

1 Preheat the oven to 190°C/375°F/ Gas 5. Grease and line a 23cm/9in sandwich cake tin. Place the eggs and caster sugar in a bowl and beat with a hand-held electric whisk until thick and mousse-like. (When the whisk is lifted, a trail should remain on the surface of the mixture for at least 15 seconds.)

NUTRITION NOTES

Per portion:
Energy	244 Kcals/1023kJ
Fat	4.05g
Saturated Fat	1.71g
Cholesterol	77.95mg
Fibre	1.50g

2 Sift the flour and cinnamon over the egg mixture and fold in with a large spoon. Pour into the prepared tin and bake for 25–30 minutes or until the cake springs back when lightly pressed. Turn the cake on to a wire rack to cool.

3 To make the filling, peel, core and slice three of the apples and put them in a saucepan. Add 30ml/2 tbsp of the honey and the water. Cover and cook over a gentle heat for about 10 minutes. Add the sultanas and cinnamon, stir well, replace the lid and leave to cool.

4 Put the soft cheese in a bowl with the remaining honey, the fromage frais and half the lemon juice. Beat until the mixture is smooth.

5 Halve the cake horizontally, place the bottom half on a board and drizzle over any liquid from the apples. Spread with two-thirds of the cheese mixture, then top with the apple filling. Fit the top of the cake in place.

6 Swirl the remaining cheese mixture over the top of the sponge. Core and slice the remaining apple, sprinkle with lemon juice and use to decorate the edge of the cake. Brush the apple with the apricot glaze and place mint sprigs on top, to decorate.

COOK'S TIP
Apricot glaze is useful for brushing over any kind of fresh fruit topping or filling. Place a few spoonfuls of apricot jam in a small pan along with a squeeze of lemon juice. Heat the jam, stirring until it is melted and runny. Pour the melted jam into a wire sieve set over a bowl. Stir the jam with a wooden spoon to help it go through. Return the strained jam to the pan. Keep the glaze warm until needed.

OATY CRISPS

These biscuits are very crisp and crunchy – ideal to serve with morning coffee.

INGREDIENTS

Makes 18
175g/6oz/1¾ cups rolled oats
75g/3oz/½ cup light muscovado
   sugar
1 egg
60ml/4 tbsp sunflower oil
30ml/2 tbsp malt extract

NUTRITION NOTES

Per portion:
Energy	86Kcals/360kJ
Fat	3.59g
Saturated Fat	0.57g
Cholesterol	10.7mg
Fibre	0.66g

1 Preheat the oven to 190°C/375°F/ Gas 5. Lightly grease two baking sheets. Mix the rolled oats and sugar in a bowl, breaking up any lumps in the sugar. Add the egg, sunflower oil and malt extract, mix well, then leave to soak for 15 minutes.

2 Using a teaspoon, place small heaps of the mixture well apart on the prepared baking sheets. Press the heaps into 7.5cm/3in rounds with the back of a dampened fork.

3 Bake the biscuits for 10–15 minutes until golden brown. Leave them to cool for 1 minute, then remove with a palette knife and cool on a wire rack.

COOK'S TIP
To give these biscuits a coarser texture, substitute jumbo oats for some or all of the rolled oats. Once cool, store the biscuits in an airtight container to keep them as crisp and fresh as possible.

DROP SCONES

These little scones are delicious spread with jam.

INGREDIENTS

Makes 18
225g/8oz/2 cups self-raising flour
2.5ml/¹/₂ tsp salt
15ml/1 tbsp caster sugar
1 egg, beaten
300ml/¹/₂ pint/1¹/₄ cups skimmed milk
oil, for frying

1 Preheat a griddle, heavy-based frying pan or an electric frying pan. Sift the flour and salt into a mixing bowl. Stir in the sugar and make a well in the centre.

2 Add the egg and half the milk, then gradually incorporate the surrounding flour to make a smooth batter. Beat in the remaining milk.

3 Lightly oil the griddle or pan. Drop tablespoons of the batter on to the surface, leaving them until they bubble and the bubbles begin to burst.

4 Turn the drop scones over with a palette knife and cook until the underside is golden brown. Keep the cooked drop scones warm and moist by wrapping them in a clean napkin while cooking successive batches.

NUTRITION NOTES	
Per portion:	
Energy	64Kcals/270kJ
Fat	1.09g
Saturated Fat	0.2g
Cholesterol	11.03mg
Fibre	0.43g

COOK'S TIP
For savoury scones, add 2 chopped spring onions and 15ml/1 tbsp of freshly grated Parmesan cheese. Serve with cottage cheese.

INDEX